COLONIAL HOUSES

"HOPE LODGE." WHITEMARSH. PENNSYLVANIA

COLONIAL HOUSES

PHILADELPHIA

PRE-REVOLUTIONARY PERIOD

by PHILIP B. WALLACE

with measured drawings by

M . LUTHER MILLER

introduction by

JOSEPH HERGESHEIMER

BONANZA BOOKS · NEW YORK, N. Y.

Dedicated to

"The Pennsylvania Society of the Colonial Dames of
America," for its patriotic interest in the preservation of the Colonial Houses of Philadelphia.

To the Pennsylvania Society of the Colonial Dames of America,
I am indebted for the use of the photographs of "Stenton"; the Metro-
politan Museum of Art of New York and Fiske Kimball, Esq., for
the use of the interiors of the Powel house, Philadelphia; William
Degn, Esq., "Hope Lodge"; Welsh Strawbridge, Esq., "Graeme
Park"; Erling H. Pedersen, Esq., "The Cliffs"; D. T. V. Hunton,
Esq., "Woodford"; Fritz Pflug, Esq., "Belmont"; Miss Lydia Morris,
"Cedar Grove," and Charles C. Whitenack, Esq., of the Penn-
sylvania Museum for their interest and assistance in presenting the
various houses.

PHILIP B. WALLACE.

Philadelphia
March 1931

Introduction

I met Philip B. Wallace a number of years ago when he was making the photographs for a book called "From An Old House." More than once, when he was making his pictures, I got annoyed at what seemed to me his illimitable slowness. Nothing escaped his attention—every visible architectural detail, every faint passage of light, all the properties of his camera and plates, were constantly in his mind. I used to hope he would forget something. He never did. Then, when I saw the photographs he had taken, I realized that he had not been slow at all. He had been careful with that minute carefulness that marks all good difficult work. His work was good, among other reasons, because he was careful. Patient. He owned the best of tempers with cornices and reflections and clouds. More than that, of course, he had a deep and inexhaustible affection for the things that occupied his mind. Lovely and peaceful things secure with the past. Old wainscoting and glass faintly lavender from a long subjection to the sun. He knew about them—in the only way that is important—by instinct.

He was, I thought, very fortunate to be interested in such subjects and such a pursuit. In a less devoted manner they had brought me a great deal of happy peacefulness. Early American houses. The existence in the Colonies and the first American Federation, the—more or less loosely—United States. Unfortunately I wrote about them; a hundred inescapable complications made my occupation with them not only difficult but practically impossible; Mr. Wallace's concern with the beginnings of his land was simpler and more direct. He thought about his subjects and then made pictures of them. He made pictures that would not only be lovely but were invariably truthful. There, forever, were the windows and doors, the facades, he celebrated. Perishable, finally, he made them in spirit anyhow imperishable. That, his records, was what those things actually were. Fixed, as I have said, for generations to study and to own.

The United States Mr. Wallace was concerned with was, even in the most remote and pastoral places, disappearing. Month by month, almost day by day, better roads, laid in concrete, were taking the place of the old country lanes with, in spring, their banks dark with violets. Day by day, it seemed, the cities were reaching out into the country with their hideous and inappropriate houses, suburbs of bungalows and villas. People built such dwellings, they lived in them, because they were the shape of the times; one unfortunate design was copied from another and multiplied out of count. Lovely serene buildings were torn down, to make way for the villas and bungalows, without any faint realization of the fatality that ignoble destruction was bringing about. No one, now, it appeared, knew what an appropriate and handsome structure was. I am not referring, sentimentally, to the life and habits, the mere appearance, of the past, but to the intrinsic and practically timeless value of line and purpose and mass; I am engaged with the effect they have on the human spirit.

I am not even, in an exact sense, patriotic. The stone farmhouses, for instance, of eastern Pennsylvania were not fine because they were built on American soil; the America they formed was created by their honesty of construction and correct proportion. Their honesty and correctness. The houses built now are neither honest in material nor correct in design. Men, then, were more intelligent about such things; they had less and, for that reason, demanded more. They built, more or less, with the help of their scattered neighbors, the dwellings they proposed to live in. Field stone and oak and white pine and a mortar harder than cement. The houses, when made of brick, were made of a brick properly, honestly, burned; the iron work was so finely wrought that it defied rust.

This was before the more obvious advantages of the machine age had arrived; before the present ingenious substitutes for oak and white pine—felt and spurious tin and composition boards. The materials of the past, like all intrinsically fine things, had a fineness in addition to integrity—they were beautiful. Especially when they were combined beautifully, with hand-made nails and oak pegs. The earlier white paint, curious to remark, seemed to have white lead in it. What there was of it—not very much in the farmhouses—stayed white. Yes, the houses of, say, the first quarter of the Eighteenth Century, in Pennsylvania, were as graceful as they were sound. Their thick walls of field stone were, on the surface, more ingratiating than any marble or coldly worked granite. Such houses, remember, were set in little green valleys, beside a stream; the spring house was built over the stream, a cool dark interior of stone and running water; and there was an apple orchard on the southern slope. Ploughed fields, Indian corn, groves of chestnut trees and maples, surrounded the dwelling.

That, fortunately or unfortunately, has gone; a little, a few lovely houses, remain for a few years longer; but, because of Mr. Wallace's particular care and ability and affection, they cannot, like so many others, utterly vanish. He has kept them in his pictures. He has preserved, in his own satisfactory manner, them and the houses of earlier, and different, cities. A city of tranquil streets and locust trees in rows and squares, commons, with their town pumps. Brick facades with orderly prim sets of steps at the doors and ornamental iron rails. Flower-like iron foot scrapers. Narrow brick sidewalks or none and high stepping stones across the streets. Dwellings, in the heart of the city, surrounded by lawns. All that Mr. Wallace has preserved, for his own happiness of mind and the pleasure of others. It is, I am convinced, more than delightful; it is immensely important. Perhaps, sometime, men will get tired of the clamor and substitutions of a mechanical age. Perhaps they will grow weary of noise, the absence of any peace or privacy.

I have only a small confidence in that, I see little hope of anything better than age upon age of apartments, of lives without homes, without the benefit of a property in the soil; and if humanity, to that limited extent, did grow in wisdom, then all that Mr. Wallace has recorded will be its testament.

The art of photography, unlike the building trade, has enormously improved since the days of Daguerre. Photographs, the photographs of Mr. Wallace, are amazingly deep in truth and in effect. They, too, show more than the surface; there is far more, in their black and white, than white and black. The spirit of places and men, of times, resides in them. The days and arts of the Colonies, of the early Nineteenth Century, are held in a lucid suspension. A great deal is made clear. A written description is infinitely less simple and appealing and direct. History, it is coming to be understood, is made out of such apparent trifles—the houses men lived in. Rooms and stairways and windows. The old traditional shapes of things.

JOSEPH HERGESHEIMER.

INDEX

"GRAEME PARK," HORSHAM, MONTGOMERY COUNTY

The house was started in 1721 and finished 1722 by Sir William Keith, Governor of Penn's Colony in 1717

MAIN ENTRANCE DOOR. "GRAEME PARK"

NORTH ELEVATION. "GRAEME PARK"

MAIN STAIRWAY. "GRAEME PARK"

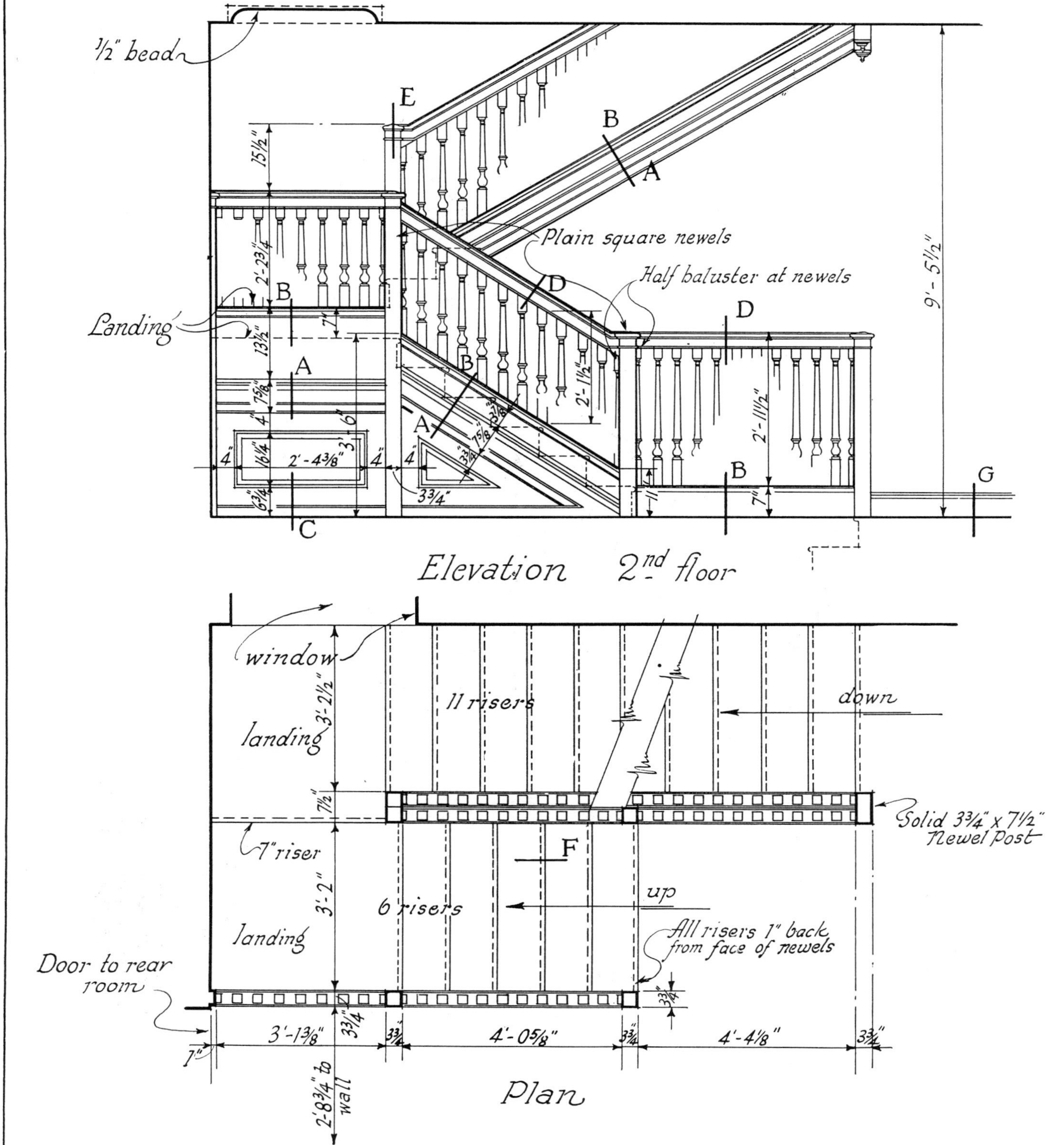
1/2" bead
E
B
A
15 1/2"
Plain square newels
Half baluster at newels
2'-2 3/4"
D
B
D
Landing
7"
13 1/2"
A
B
7 5/8"
4"
3'-6"
2'-1 1/2"
7 5/8
3 3/4
2'-11 1/2"
9'-5 1/2"
A
4"
16 1/4
2'-4 3/8"
4"
4"
3 3/4"
1"
B
7"
G
6 3/4
C
Elevation 2nd floor
window
landing
3'-2 1/2"
11 risers
down
7 1/2"
Solid 3 3/4" x 7 1/2" Newel Post
7" riser
F
up
3'-2"
6 risers
landing
All risers 1" back from face of newels
Door to rear room
3 3/4
3'-1 3/8"
3 3/4
3 3/4
4'-0 5/8"
3 3/4
4'-4 1/8"
3 3/4
7"
2'-8 3/4" to wall
Plan

Stair Details

GRAEME PARK

Horsham Pennsylvania

Scale 0 1ft. 2ft. 3ft.

No wall string to receive treads above 2nd floor. Stairs of white-oak

STAIR DETAIL. "GRAEME PARK"

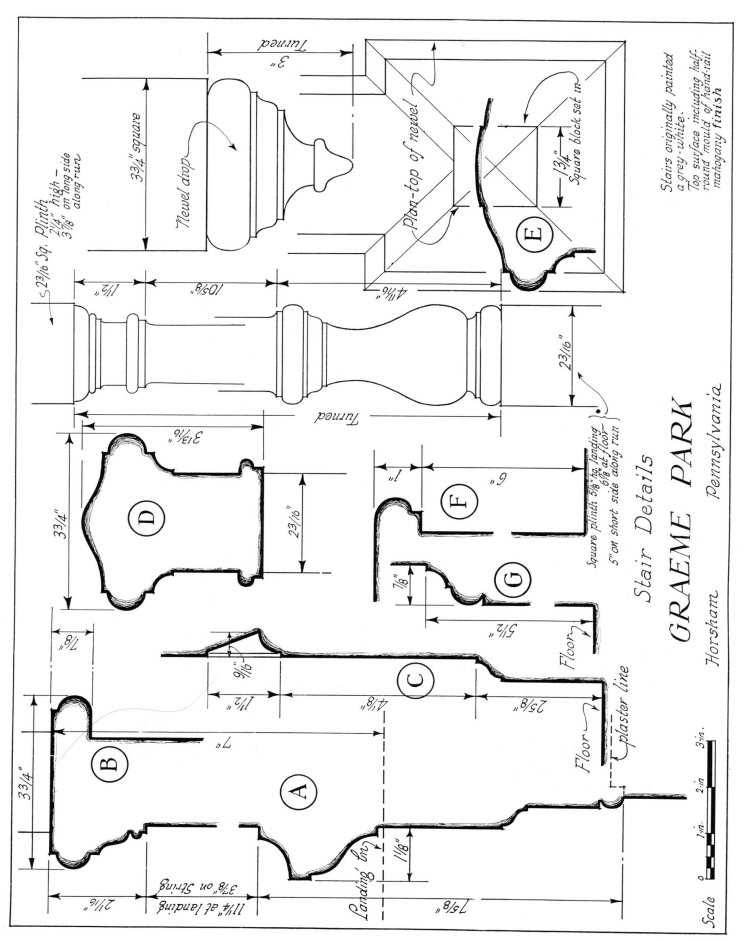

Stairs originally painted
a grey-white.
Top surface including half-
round mould of hand-rail
mahogany finish

Stair Details

GRAEME PARK

Horsham   Pennsylvania

Scale

DETAIL OF WEST ELEVATION. SECOND FLOOR PARLOR
"GRAEME PARK"

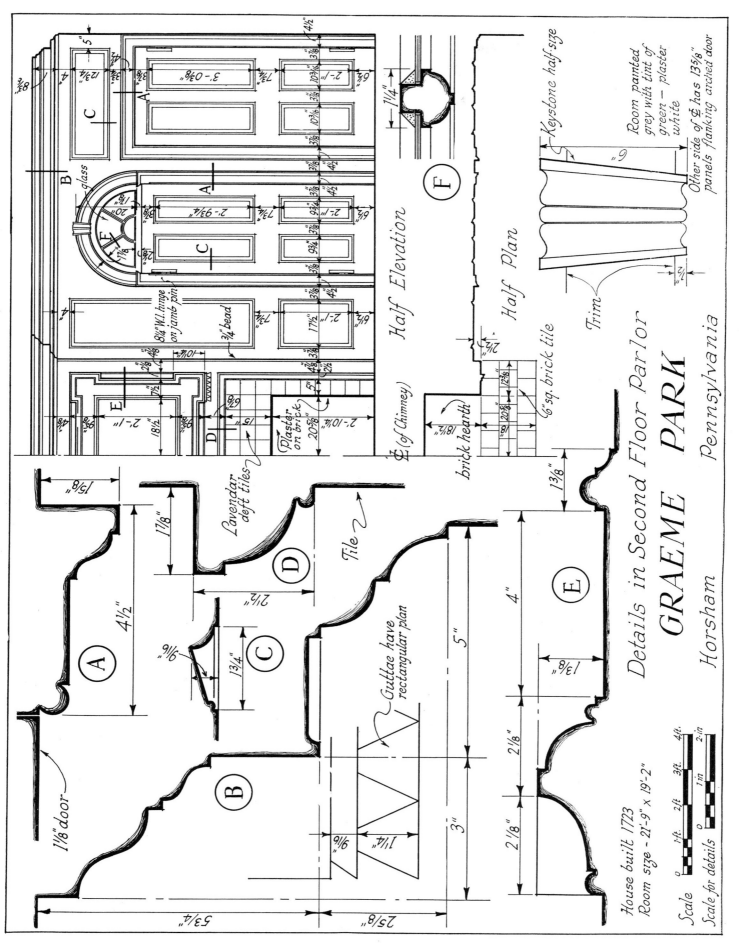

Details in Second Floor Parlor

GRAEME PARK

Horsham   Pennsylvania

House built 1723
Room size - 21'-9" x 19'-2"

Scale
Scale for details

Half Elevation

Half Plan

Keystone half-size

Room painted grey with tint of green — plaster white

Other side of £ has 13⅝" panels flanking arched door

Trim

6" sq. brick tile

brick hearth

£ (of Chimney)

Plaster on brick

Lavendar delft tiles

Tile

Guttae have rectangular plan

1⅛" door

DETAIL OF WINDOW SEAT. 'GRAEME PARK"

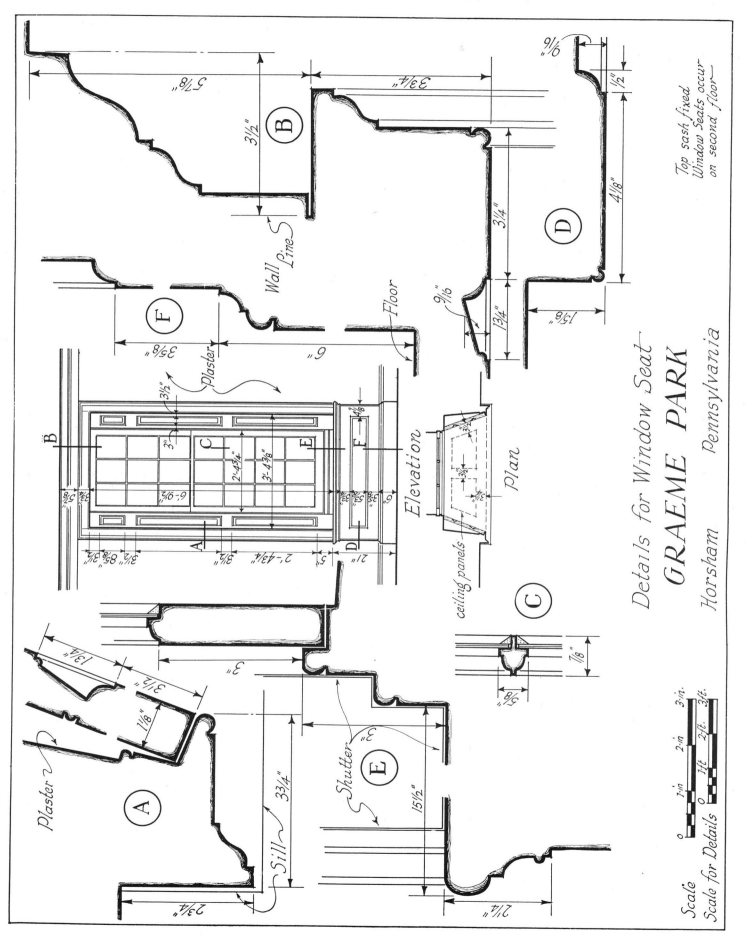

Details for Window Seat

GRAEME PARK

Horsham   Pennsylvania

Top sash fixed
Window Seats occur
on second floor

Scale

Scale for Details

DETAIL OF PANELING. EAST ELEVATION. SECOND FLOOR PARLOR
"GRAEME PARK"

FIREPLACE AND PANELING OF WEST CHAMBER. SECOND FLOOR
"GRAEME PARK"

WEST ELEVATION OF DRAWING ROOM. FIRST FLOOR
"GRAEME PARK"

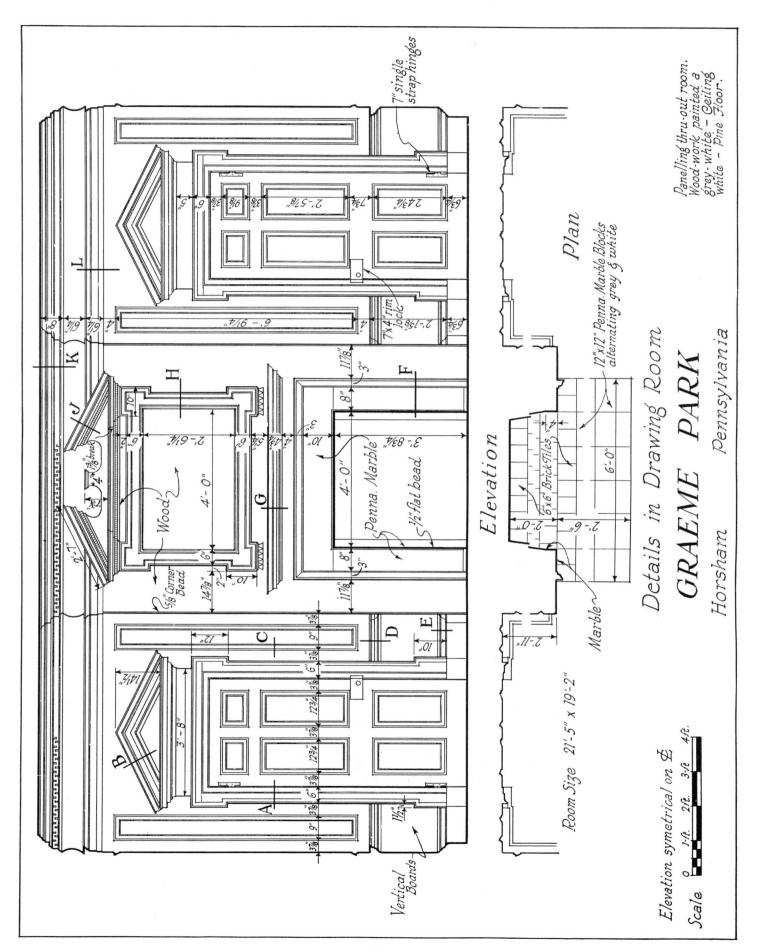

Details in Drawing Room
GRAEME PARK
Horsham   Pennsylvania

Elevation

Plan

Paneling thru-out room.
Wood-work painted a
grey-white – Ceiling
white – Pine Floor.

12"x12" Penna Marble Blocks
alternating grey & white

6x6" Brick Tiles

Penna. Marble

Room Size 21'-5" x 19'-2"

Elevation symetrical on ℄

Scale

7" single
strap hinges

Vertical
Boards

DOORWAY. DRAWING ROOM TO STAIR HALL
"GRAEME PARK"

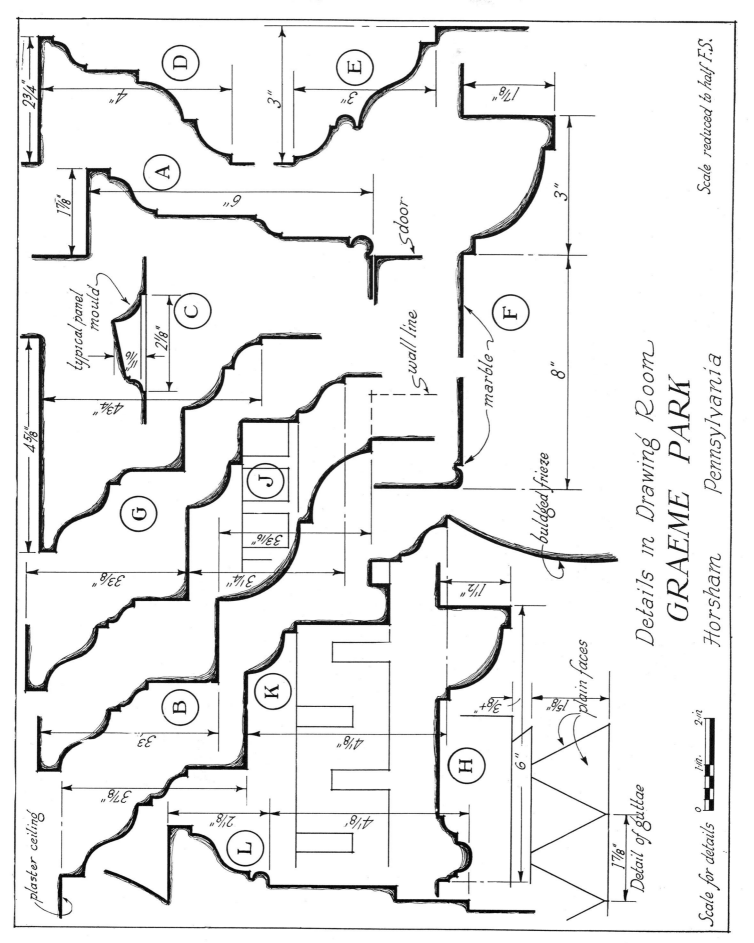

Details in Drawing Room
GRAEME PARK
Horsham   Pennsylvania

Scale reduced to half F.S.

Scale for details

WINDOW DETAIL AND SIDE WALL PANELING
DRAWING ROOM. "GRAEME PARK"

WEST ELEVATION, SHOWING WINDOW SEAT. SECOND FLOOR PARLOR

FULL ELEVATION. WEST SIDE. SECOND FLOOR PARLOR
"GRAEME PARK"

"HOPE LODGE," WHITEMARSH VALLEY
Was built in 1723 by Samuel Morris, a Welsh Quaker. It is typical of brick structures built in this section
of the Colonies.

WINDOW DETAIL. "HOPE LODGE"

ENTRANCE HALL. "HOPE LODGE"

ENTRANCE HALL TO NORTH PARLOR
"HOPE LODGE"

DETAIL. ENTRANCE HALL
"HOPE LODGE"

ENTRANCE HALL DETAIL
"HOPE LODGE"

DETAIL OF DOORWAY. ENTRANCE HALL
"HOPE LODGE"

DOORWAY TO DINING ROOM
"HOPE LODGE"

VISTA FROM NORTH PARLOR
"HOPE LODGE"

TILES. "HOPE LODGE"

TILES. "WHITBY HALL."

DOOR DETAIL. HALLWAY INTO SOUTH PARLOR
"HOPE LODGE"

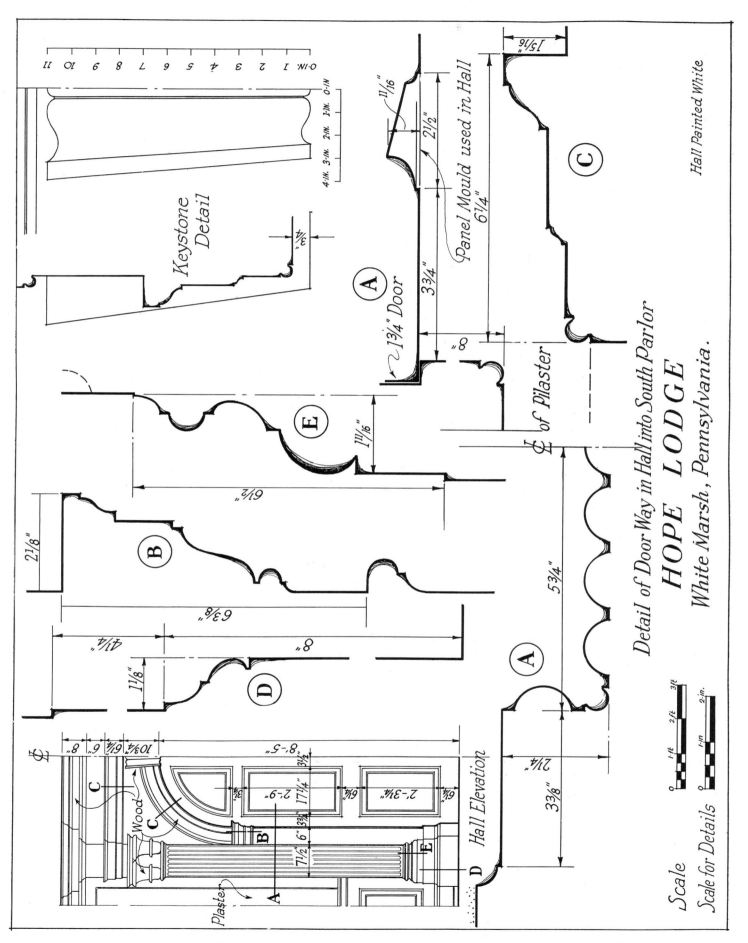

Keystone Detail

Panel Mould used in Hall

Detail of Door-Way in Hall into South Parlor

HOPE LODGE

White Marsh, Pennsylvania.

Hall Painted White

Scale

Scale for Details

Hall Elevation

FIREPLACE AND PANELING. NORTH PARLOR
"HOPE LODGE"

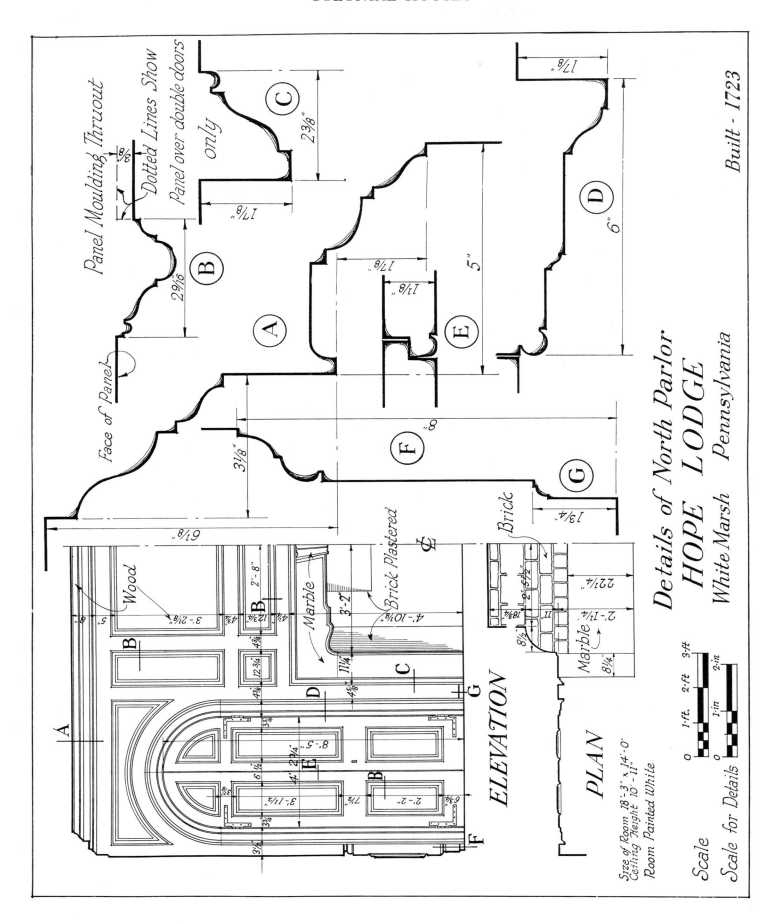

Details of North Parlor
HOPE LODGE   White Marsh   Pennsylvania

Built - 1723

ELEVATION

PLAN

Size of Room 18'-3" x 14'-0"
Ceiling Height 10'-11"
Room Painted White

Scale
Scale for Details

FIREPLACE. NORTH PARLOR
"HOPE LODGE"

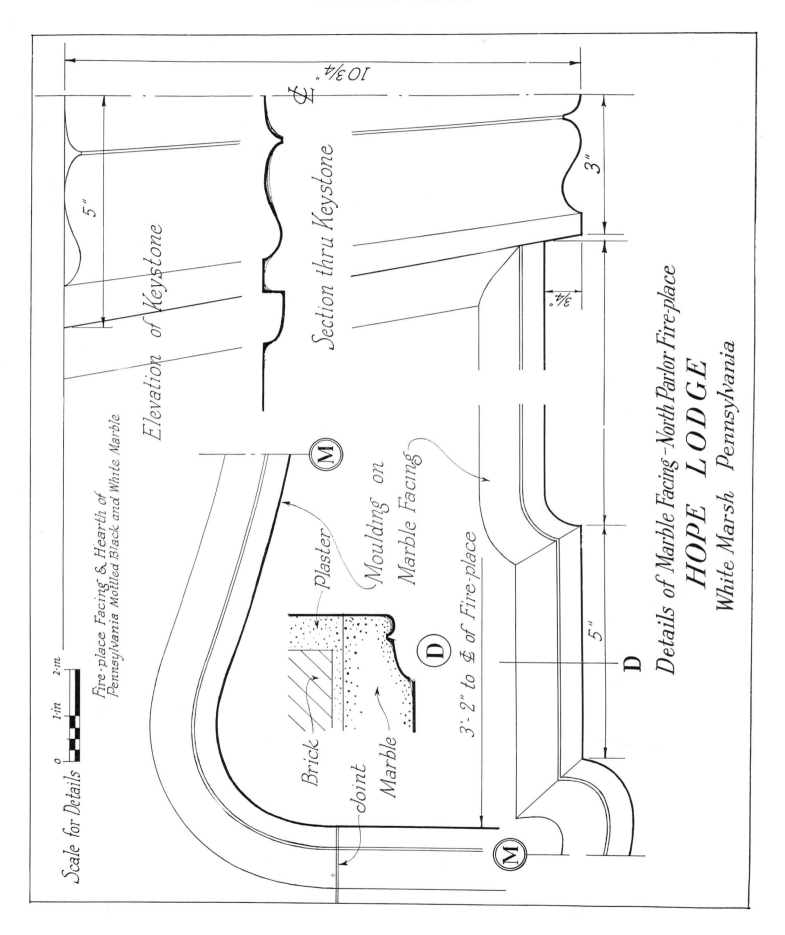

Scale for Details

2-in.

1-in.

0

Fire-place Facing & Hearth of
Pennsylvania Mottled Black and White Marble

Elevation of Keystone

Section thru Keystone

10 3/4."

5"

3"

3/4"

Plaster

Moulding on
Marble Facing

Brick

Joint

Marble

M

D

M

D

3'-2" to ₵ of Fire-place

5"

Details of Marble Facing - North Parlor Fire-place

HOPE LODGE

White Marsh Pennsylvania

DETAIL OF DOORWAY. DINING ROOM
"HOPE LODGE"

STAIRWAY. FIRST FLOOR
"HOPE LODGE"

STAIR LANDING
"HOPE LODGE"

DETAIL OF WAINSCOT. STAIRWAY
"HOPE LODGE"

BEDROOM. "HOPE LODGE"

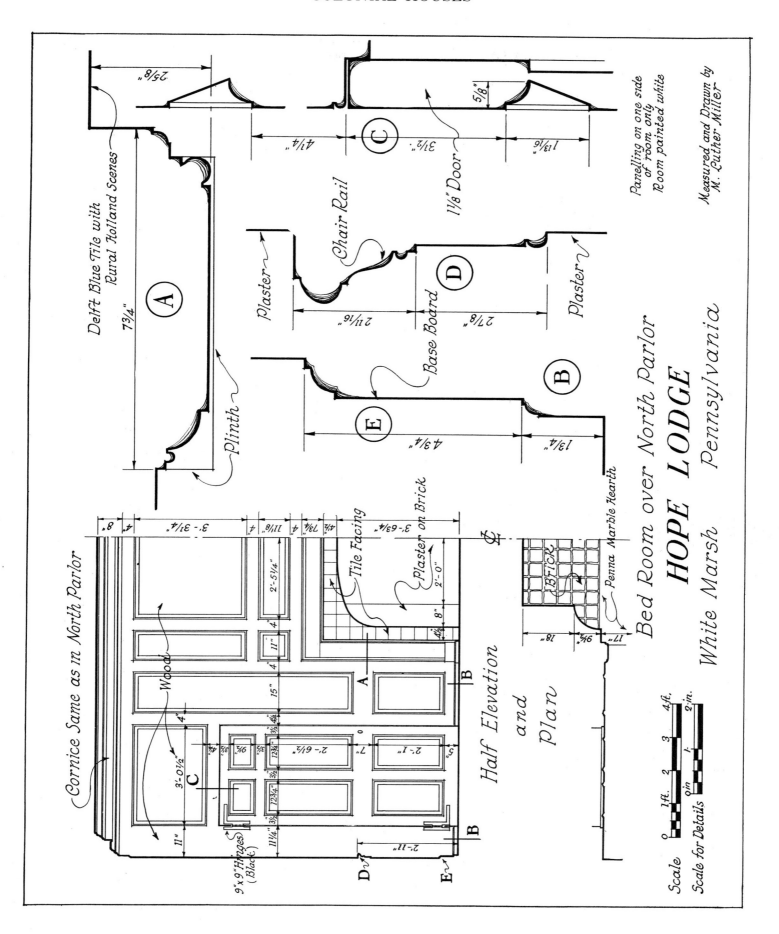

Delft Blue Tile with
Rural Holland Scenes

A

7¾"

Plinth

2⅝"

C

4¼"

3½"

Chair Rail

1⅛" Door

5/8"

1³⁄₁₆"

Plaster

D

Base Board

2¹¹⁄₁₆"

2⅞"

Plaster

Plaster

B

E

4¾"

1¾"

Penna Marble Hearth

Panelling on one side
of room only
Room painted white

Measured and Drawn by
M. Luther Miller

Cornice Same as in North Parlor

8"

4"

3'-3¼"

11⅛"

7¾"

4½"

Wood

2'-5¼"

11"

4"

15"

4"

4½"

3½"

¾₆"

3½"

4½"

12¾"

2'-6½"

7"

0

2'-1"

5"

3'-0½"

C

11"

11¼"

3½"

12¾"

9×9" Hinges
(Black)

D

2'-11"

B

Tile Facing

Plaster on Brick

2'-0"

8"

4½"

A

3'-6¾"

B

BRICK

18"

9½"

17"

Penna Marble Hearth

E

B

Half Elevation
and
Plan

Bed Room over North Parlor

HOPE LODGE   Pennsylvania

White Marsh

Scale   0   1ft.   2   3   4ft.

Scale for Details   0 in.   1   2 in.

DETAIL OF WINDOW SEAT
"HOPE LODGE"

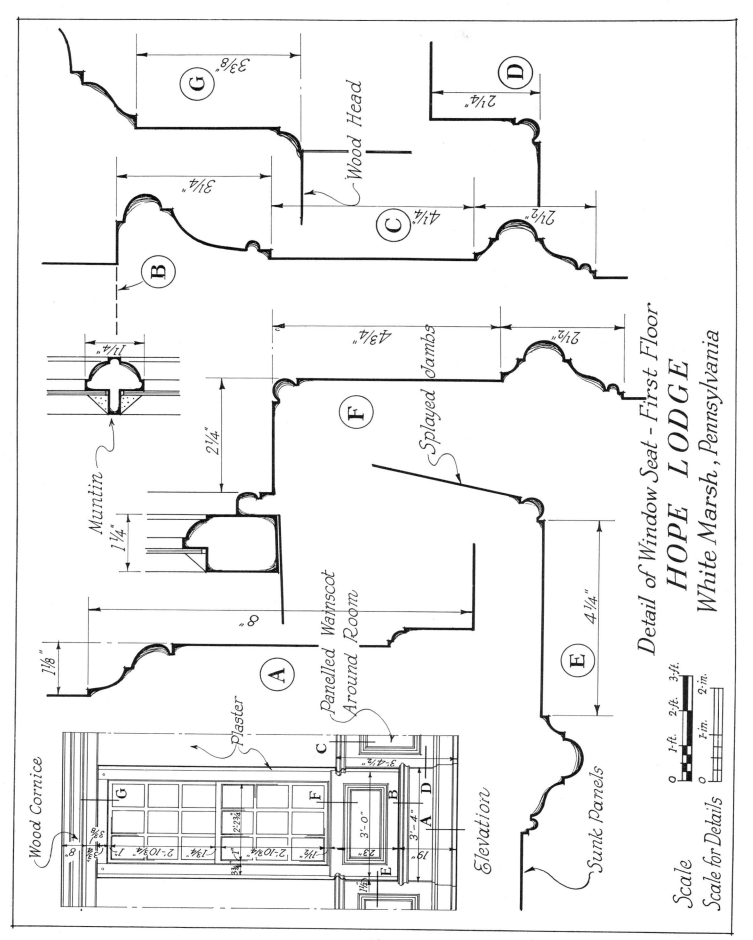

Detail of Window Seat - First Floor
HOPE LODGE
White Marsh, Pennsylvania

DETAIL OF KITCHEN. "HOPE LODGE"

"STENTON," GERMANTOWN ROAD

The home of James Logan, Secretary to Wm. Penn, built in 1728. It was saved from destruction by fire at the hands of British Troops 1777, and occupied both by Washington and Howe as headquarters.

NORTH ELEVATION. "STENTON"

GARDEN PORCH. "STENTON"

VIEW FROM THE EAST. "STENTON"

MAIN ENTRANCE DOOR. "STENTON"

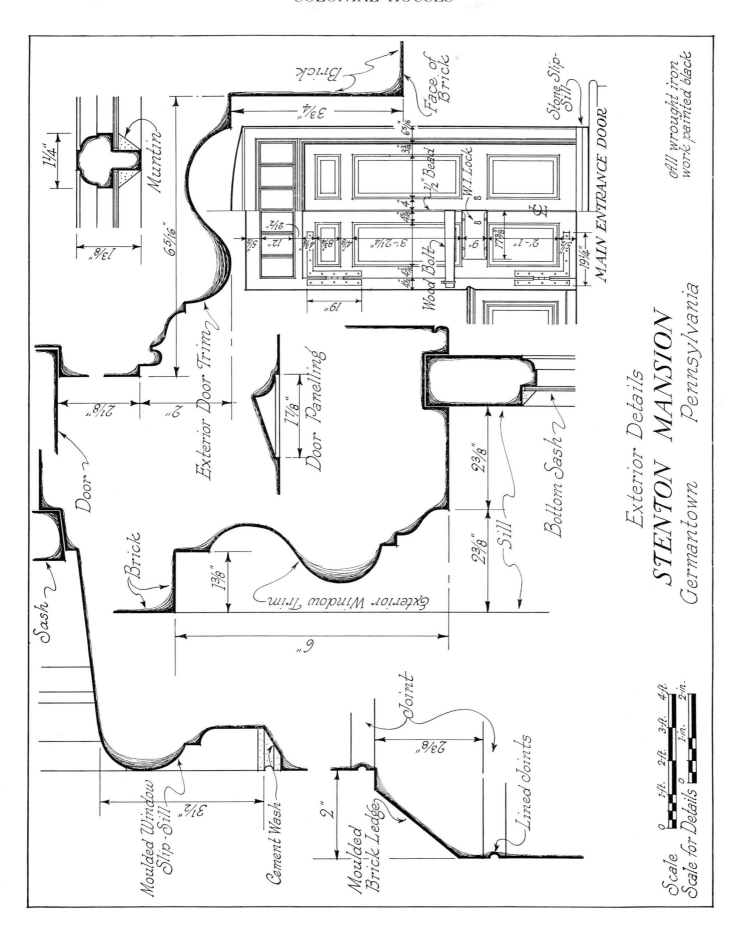

Exterior Details

STENTON MANSION
Germantown   Pennsylvania

VIEW FROM STAIR HALL. "STENTON"

ENTRANCE HALL TO STAIRWAY. "STENTON"

DOORWAY TO STAIR HALL. "STENTON"

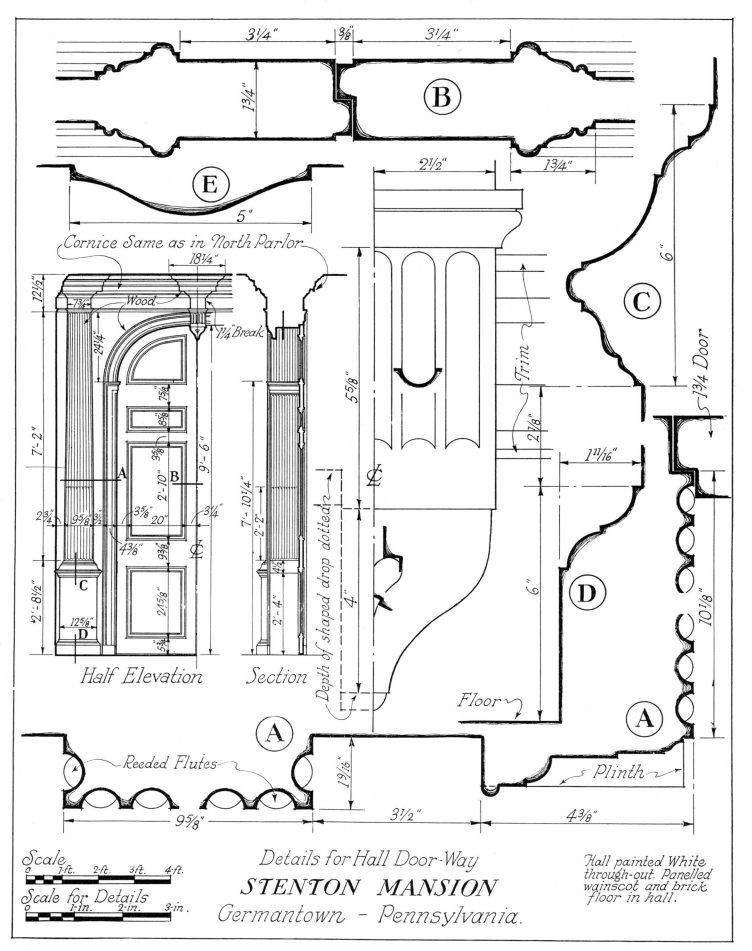

B

E

3¼" ⅜" 3¼"

13¾"

2½" 13¾"

6"

C

1¾ Door

Cornice Same as in North Parlor

18¼"

12½"

7¾" Wood

24¼" 1¼ Break

7-2"

A B

7½"

8⅝" 75⁄8

3⅝"

9-6"

2'-10"

2¾" 95⁄8 3½

3⅝" 20" 3¼"

4⅜"

938"

C

2'-8½"

12⅝"

D

2'-4 15⁄8"

53⁄4

Half Elevation

Section

7-10¼"

2'-2"

4½"

Depth of shaped drop dotted

55⁄8"

4"

Trim

2⅛"

1 11⁄16"

6"

D

6"

Floor

A

Plinth

10⅛"

A

Reeded Flutes

19⁄16"

95⁄8"

3½"

4⅜"

Scale
0 1-ft. 2-ft. 3ft. 4-ft.

Scale for Details
0 1-in. 2-in. 3-in.

Details for Hall Door-Way
STENTON MANSION
Germantown - Pennsylvania.

Hall painted White
through-out. Panelled
wainscot and brick
floor in hall.

53

FIREPLACE. ENTRANCE HALL. "STENTON"

DETAIL DOORWAY. "STENTON"

VISTA TO STAIRWAY. "STENTON"

DOOR DETAIL. ENTRANCE HALL
"STENTON"

FIREPLACE AND PANELING. NORTH PARLOR
"STENTON"

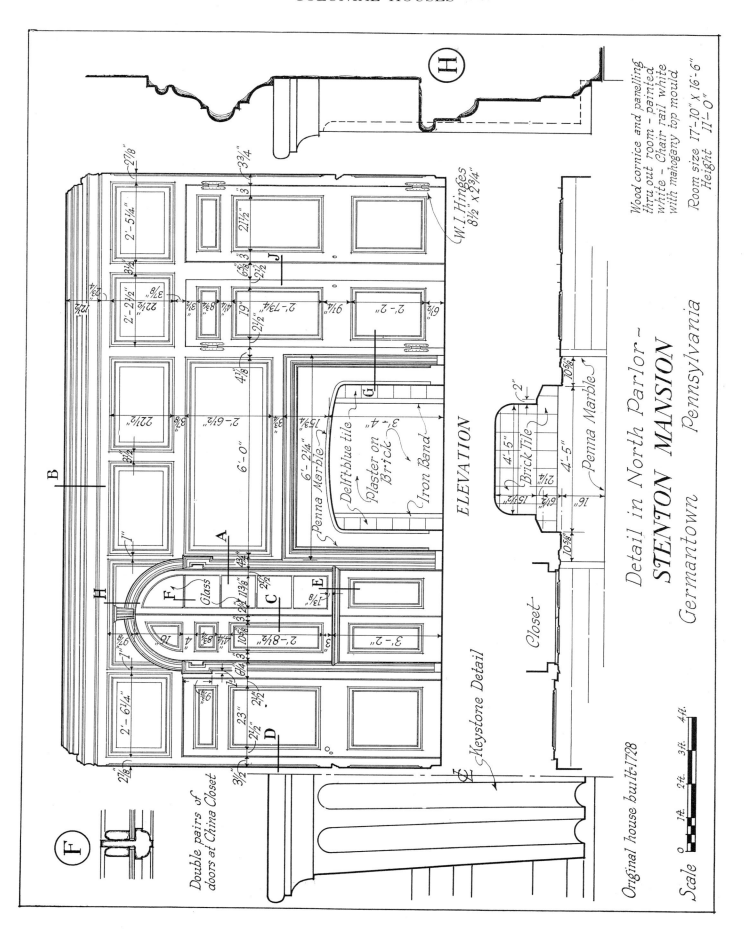

Detail in North Parlor ~
STENTON MANSION
Germantown   Pennsylvania

ELEVATION

Wood cornice and panelling
thru out room – painted
white – Chair rail white
with mahogany top mould

Room size 17'-10" X 16'-6"
Height 11'-0"

Double pairs of
doors at China Closet

Original house built 1728

Scale

WINDOW SEAT. NORTH PARLOR
"STENTON"

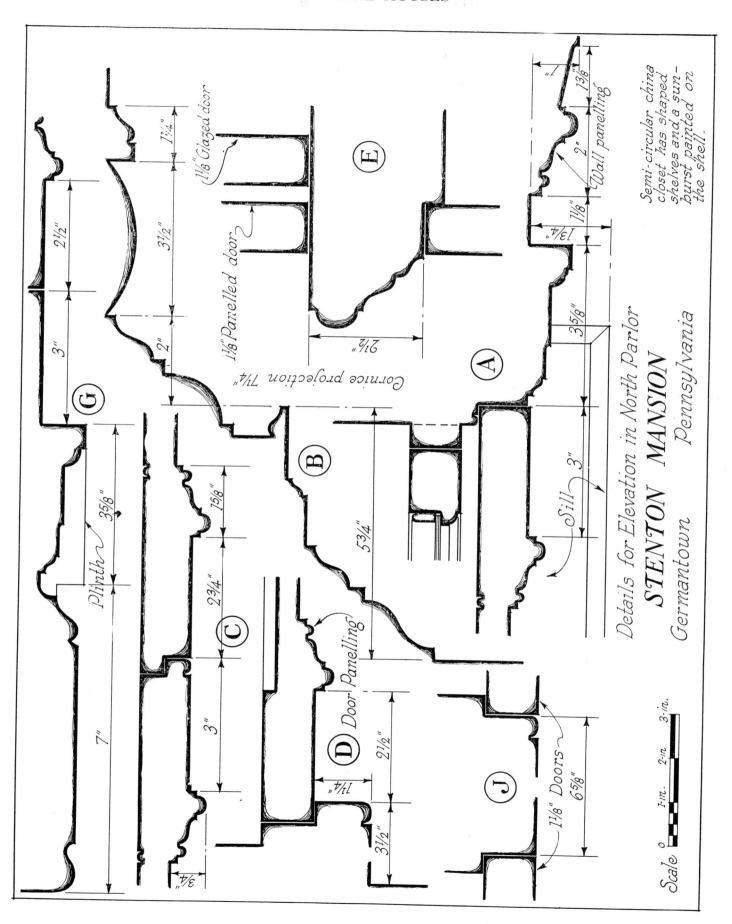

Details for Elevation in North Parlor
STENTON MANSION
Germantown   Pennsylvania

Semi-circular china closet has shaped shelves and a sunburst painted on the shell.

Scale

ELEVATION IN NORTH PARLOR. "STENTON"

CHINA CLOSET. NORTH PARLOR. "STENTON"

ELEVATION. DINING ROOM. "STENTON"

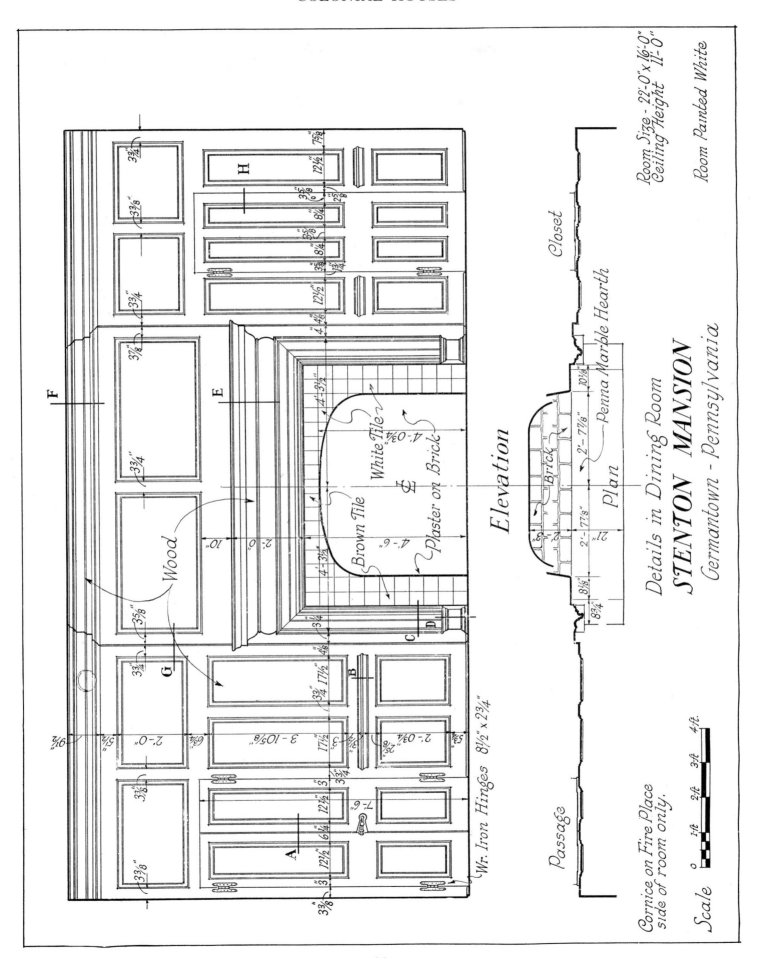

Details in Dining Room

STENTON MANSION

Germantown - Pennsylvania

Room Size - 22'-0" x 16'-0"
Ceiling Height 11'-0"

Room Painted White

Elevation

Plan

Passage

Closet

Penna Marble Hearth

Brick

Plaster on Brick

White Tile

Brown Tile

Wood

Wr. Iron Hinges 8½" x 2¾"

Cornice on Fire Place side of room only.

Scale

LOOKING INTO DINING ROOM
"STENTON"

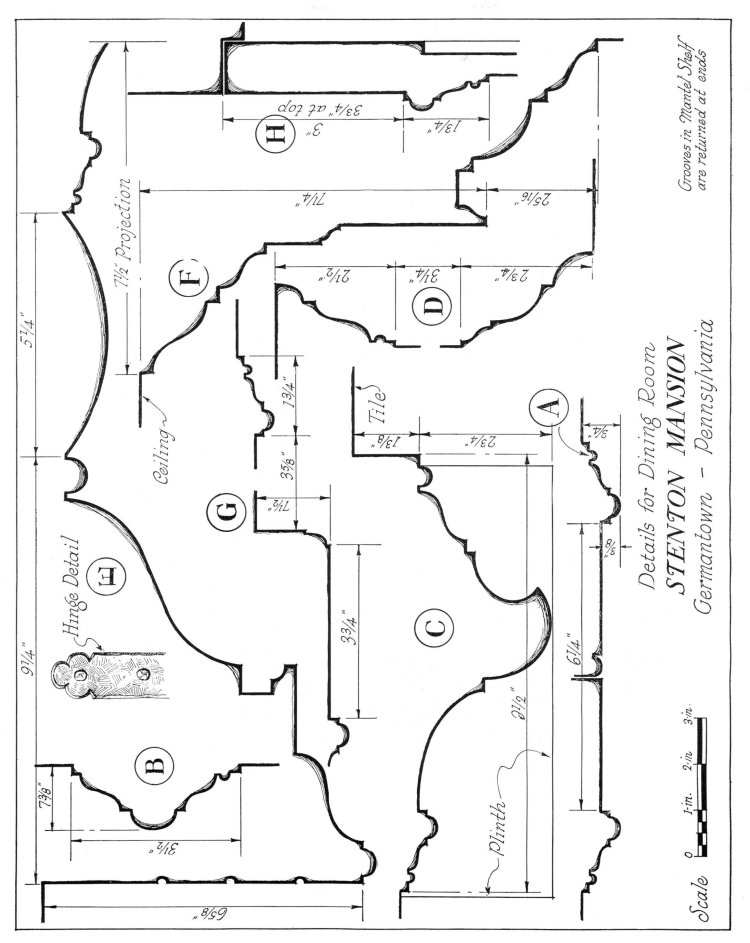

Details for Dining Room
STENTON MANSION
Germantown – Pennsylvania

Scale

Grooves in Mantel Shelf
are returned at ends

STAIRWAY. "STENTON"

BEDROOM FIREPLACE. "STENTON"

FIREPLACE. WEST BEDROOM. "STENTON"

DOORWAY. WEST BEDROOM. "STENTON"

FIREPLACE AND PANELING. WEST BEDROOM
"STENTON"

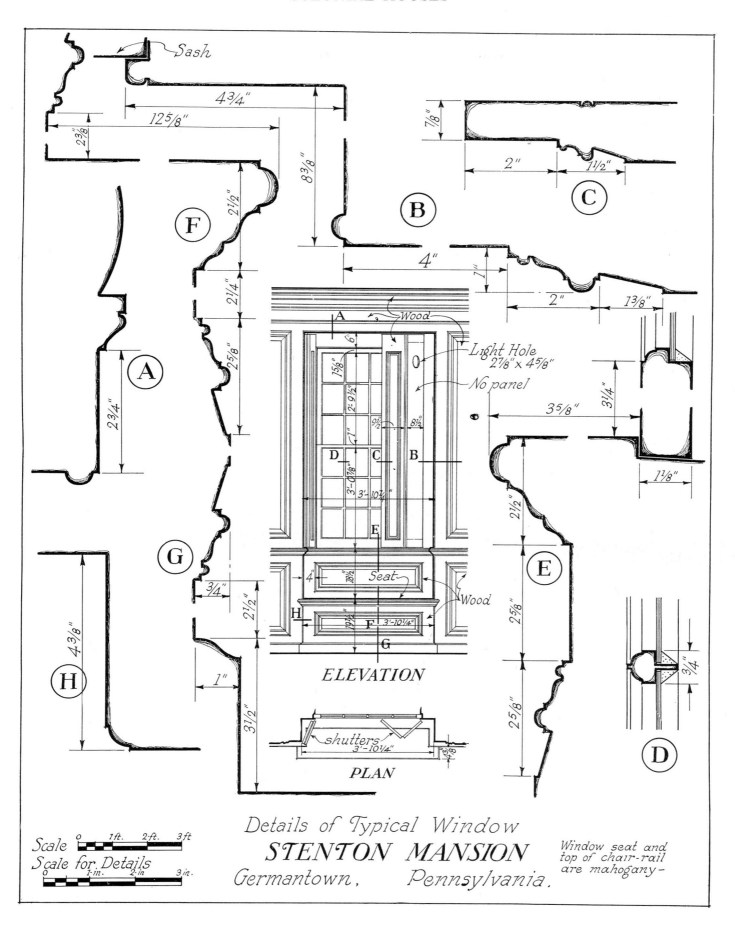

Sash

F · A · G · H · B · C · E · D

ELEVATION

Wood · **Light Hole 2⅞" x 4⅝"** · **No panel**

Seat · **Wood**

PLAN

shutters 3'-10¼"

Scale 0 1 ft. 2 ft. 3 ft.
Scale for Details 0 1 in. 2 in. 3 in.

Details of Typical Window
STENTON MANSION
Germantown, Pennsylvania.

Window seat and
top of chair-rail
are mahogany—

73

FIREPLACE. BEDROOM. THIRD FLOOR
"STENTON"

FIREPLACE. SMALL BEDROOM
"STENTON"

FIREPLACE AND PANELING. "HOPE LODGE"

ENTRANCE HALL DETAIL. "STENTON"

"BARTRAM HOUSE" (KINGSESSING), WEST PHILADELPHIA

Was built as an addition to a small Swedish house already on the site in 1730-31. It was later added to in 1770 (see inscriptions) by John Bartram, America's first distinguished botanist. River front elevation.

INSCRIPTION AND DATE STONE, SOUTH GABLE

INSCRIPTION UNDER SECOND FLOOR WINDOW
"BARTRAM HOUSE"

STONE DETAIL. PORCH

SQUARE COLUMN BASE. PORCH

"BARTRAM HOUSE"

DETAIL OF STONE WORK. WINDOW

DETAIL OF CARVED STONE LINTEL
"BARTRAM HOUSE"

ENTRANCE HALL. "BARTRAM HOUSE"

STAIRWAY. FIRST FLOOR
"BARTRAM HOUSE"

DETAIL. KITCHEN. "BARTRAM HOUSE"

FIRE PLACE IN KITCHEN
"BARTRAM HOUSE"

DINING ROOM TO ENTRANCE HALL

BARTRAM HOUSE"

CUPBOARD. ENTRANCE HALL

DINING ROOM FIREPLACE
"BARTRAM HOUSE"

DETAIL IN DINING ROOM
"BARTRAM HOUSE"

BED ROOM. SECOND FLOOR
"BARTRAM HOUSE"

SECOND FLOOR HALLWAY
"BARTRAM HOUSE"

"WOODFORD," FAIRMOUNT PARK

Was built by William Coleman, 1756, later passing into the hands of David Franks, a prominent Tory during the revolution.

MAIN ENTRANCE DOOR
"WOODFORD"

INTERIOR. SIDE ENTRANCE DOOR
"WOODFORD"

DETAIL IN ENTRANCE HALL
"WOODFORD"

STAIRWAY. "WOODFORD"

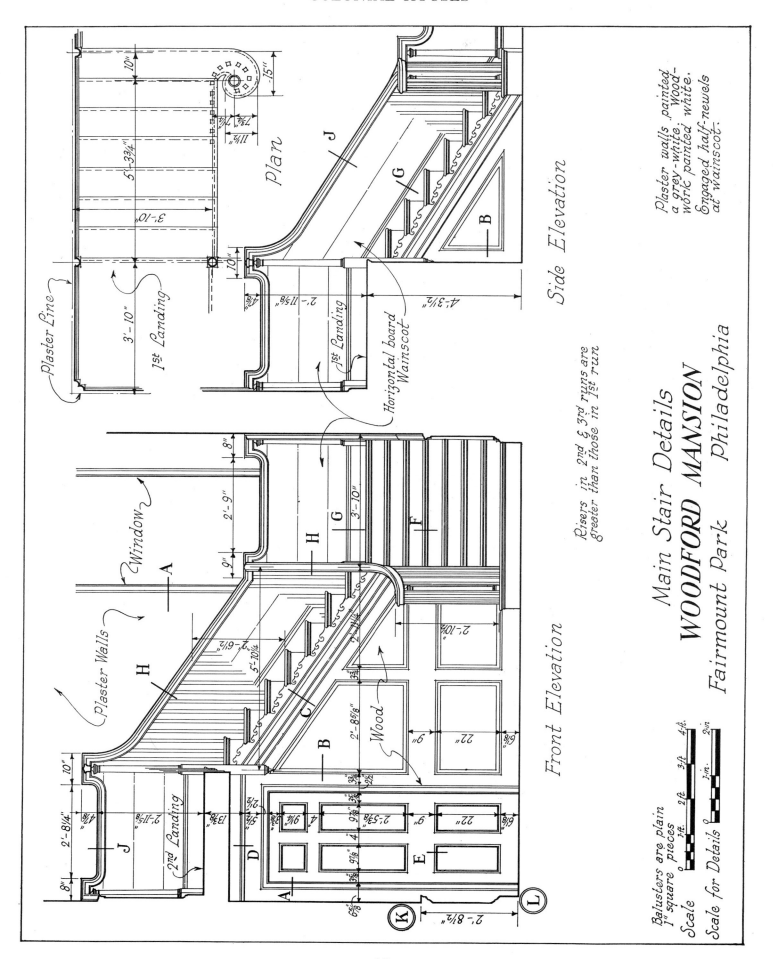

Plan

Plaster Line

1st Landing

3'-10"

Side Elevation

Horizontal board
Wainscot

1st Landing

Plaster walls painted
a grey-white. Wood-
work painted white.
Engaged half-newels
at wainscot.

Window

Plaster Walls

Front Elevation

Wood

Balusters are plain
1" square pieces

Scale

Scale for Details

Risers in 2nd & 3rd runs are
greater than those in 1st run

Main Stair Details
WOODFORD MANSION
Fairmount Park   Philadelphia

DETAIL. STAIR BRACKETS

"WOODFORD"

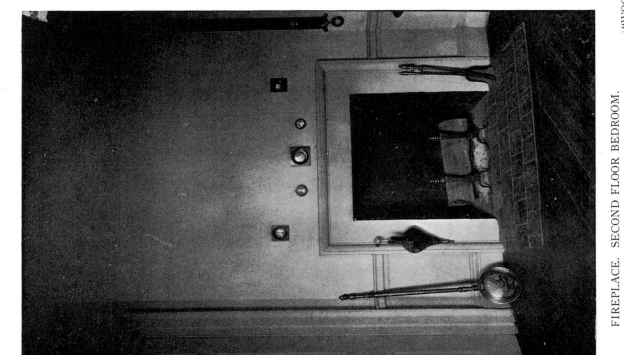

FIREPLACE. SECOND FLOOR BEDROOM.

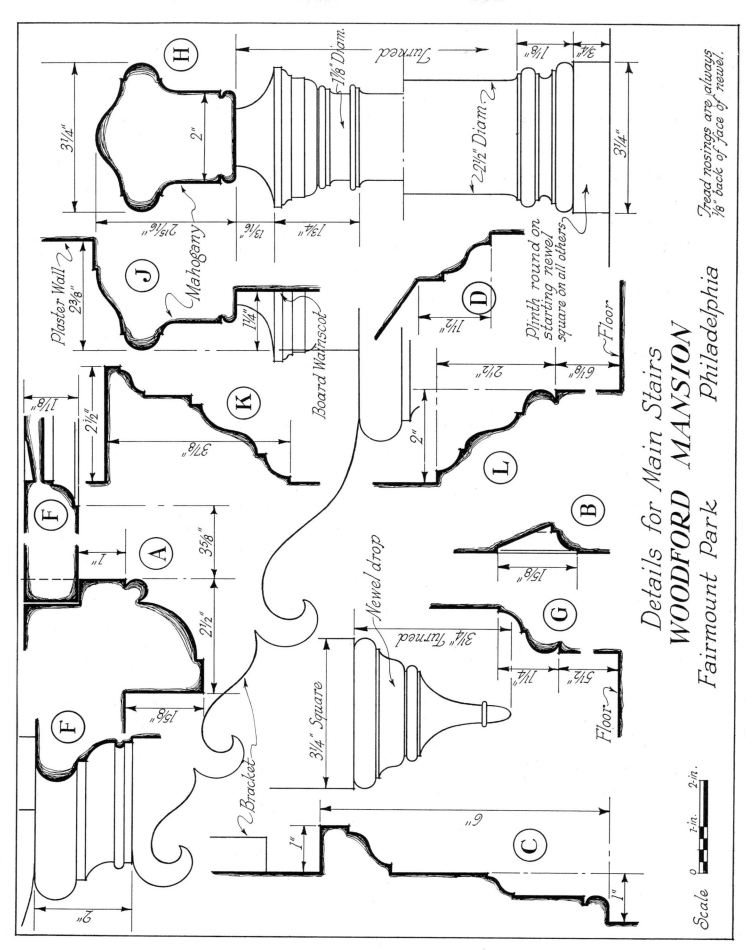

Details for Main Stairs
WOODFORD MANSION   Philadelphia
Fairmount Park

Tread nosings are always
⅛" back of face of newel.

Scale

97

LIVING ROOM. "WOODFORD"

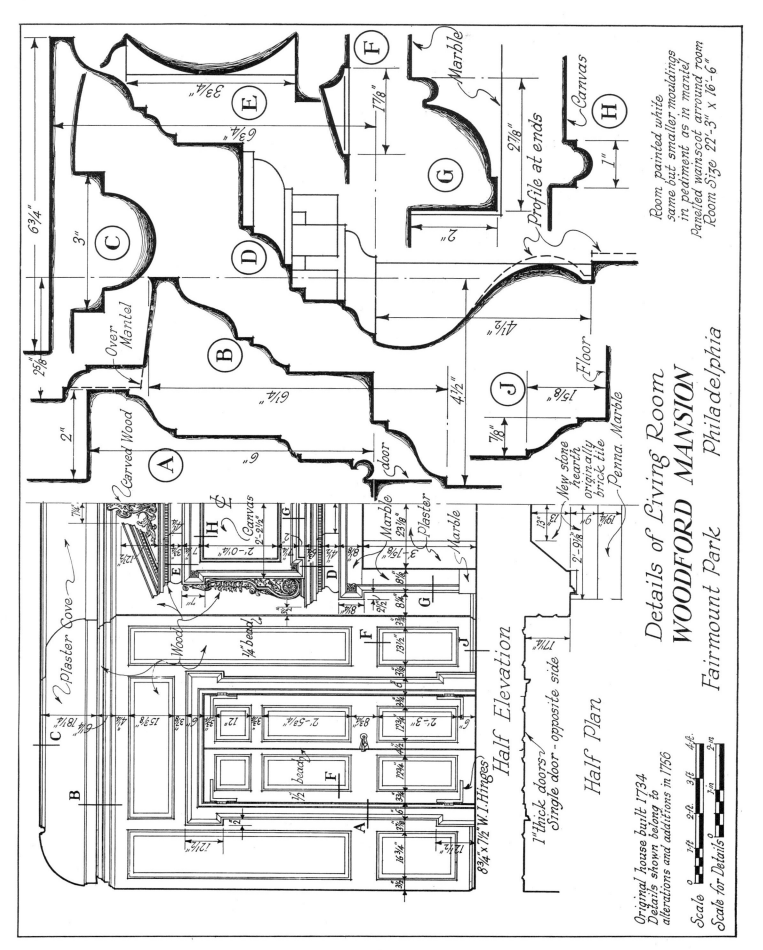

Details of Living Room
WOODFORD MANSION   Philadelphia
Fairmount Park

Room painted white
same but smaller mouldings
in pediment as in mantel
Panelled wainscot arround room
Room Size 22'-3" x 16'-6"

Half Elevation

Half Plan

Original house built 1734
Details shown belong to
alterations and additions in 1756

Scale

Scale for Details

MANTEL DETAIL

DETAIL OVER MANTEL
"WOODFORD"

DINING ROOM. "WOODFORD"

ENTRANCE HALL

DETAIL DOORWAY. LIVING ROOM

"WOODFORD"

"WHITBY HALL" (KINGSESSING), WEST PHILADELPHIA

Was built by James Coultas, Merchant Ship Owner and High Sheriff of Philadelphia from 1755 to 1758. The house was erected in 1754, being an addition to the house already on site. The building has been demolished during the last decade.

MAIN ENTRANCE DOOR
"WHITBY HALL"

PORCH DETAIL. "WHITBY HALL"

INTERIOR ELEVATION. MAIN ENTRANCE DOOR
"WHITBY HALL"

STAIRWAY. FIRST FLOOR
"WHITBY HALL"

DETAIL OF NEWEL STAIRWAY
"WHITBY HALL"

STAIRWAY LANDING
"WHITBY HALL"

WINDOW SEAT. STAIR LANDING
"WHITBY HALL"

STAIRWAY SECOND FLOOR
"WHITBY HALL"

FIREPLACE AND PANELING. MAIN PARLOR
"WHITBY HALL"

DETAIL. FIREPLACE. MAIN PARLOR
"WHITBY HALL"

DETAIL. TOPS OF CHINA CLOSETS. MAIN PARLOR
"WHITBY HALL"

DETAIL OF DOORWAY
"WHITBY HALL"

DETAIL OF WINDOW. FIRST FLOOR. "WHITBY HALL"

DETAIL OF WINDOW. SECOND FLOOR
"WHITBY HALL"

PANELING IN BEDROOM. "WHITBY HALL"

DETAIL, STAIR LANDING

"WHITBY HALL"

DETAIL IN STAIR HALL

"BELMONT" (BLACKLEY TOWNSHIP), FAIRMOUNT PARK

Here was born and died Hon. Richard Peters, Commissioner of War during the revolution. The house was built in 1742-3 by William Peters, his father. The exterior of the house has been so altered that hardly a vestige of its original self remains. Mantel in Parlor.

DOOR TO STAIR HALL
"BELMONT"

DETAIL OF NEWEL. STAIRWAY
"BELMONT"

ARCHWAY. SECOND FLOOR HALL
"BELMONT"

STAIR LANDING. SECOND FLOOR

"BELMONT"

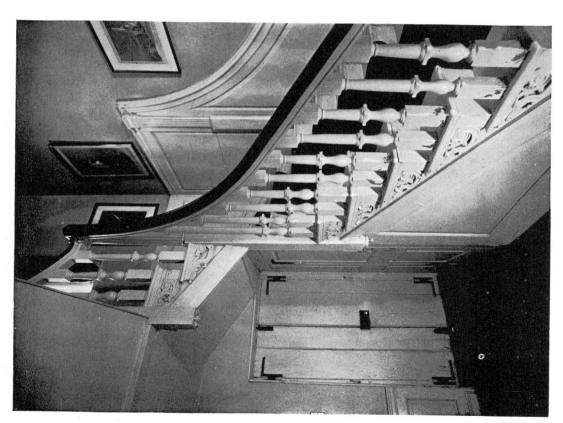

STAIR HALL

RAMP. STAIR WAINSCOT

STAIR BRACKET DETAIL
"BELMONT"

124

ELEVATION OF PARLOR. "BELMONT"

DOORWAY.   PARLOR

"BELMONT"

DETAIL OF DOORWAY

PLASTER DETAILS. CEILING IN PARLOR
"BELMONT"

MANTEL DETAIL. SECOND FLOOR BEDROOM

DETAIL OF PEDIMENT OVER MANTEL. PARLOR
"BELMONT"

MANTEL. BEDROOM. SECOND FLOOR
"BELMONT"

CORNER FIREPLACE. SECOND FLOOR BEDROOM

"BELMONT"

FIREPLACE. BODY SERVANTS' ROOM

"CEDAR GROVE" (HARROGATE), FRANKFORD

Was built in 1748 by Elizabeth Coates Paschall, widow of Joseph Paschall. The original two room house was added to at later dates. The house is now preserved in Fairmount Park.

FIRE PLACE. DINING ROOM
"CEDAR GROVE"

STAIRWAY TO SECOND FLOOR
"CEDAR GROVE"

FIREPLACE. FIRST FLOOR
"CEDAR GROVE"

KITCHEN FIREPLACE. "CEDAR GROVE"

BEDROOM. SECOND FLOOR
"CEDAR GROVE"

BED ROOM. SECOND FLOOR
"CEDAR GROVE"

BED ROOM. SECOND FLOOR
"CEDAR GROVE"

"MOUNT PLEASANT," FAIRMOUNT PARK

Was built by Captain John Macpherson, 1761. It is one of the most elegant country seats of its period. The grouping is impressive and it is one of the few examples in a perfect state of preservation.

EAST ELEVATION. "MOUNT PLEASANT"

MAIN ENTRANCE DOOR. "MOUNT PLEASANT"

WEST ENTRANCE DOOR. "MOUNT PLEASANT"

OUT BUILDING. "MOUNT PLEASANT"

DETAIL IN ENTRANCE HALL
"MOUNT PLEASANT"

ENTRANCE HALL. LOOKING TOWARD STAIRWAY
"MOUNT PLEASANT"

NEWEL. STAIRWAY. "MOUNT PLEASANT"

STAIR DETAIL. "MOUNT PLEASANT"

STAIR LANDING. SECOND FLOOR. "MOUNT PLEASANT"

SECOND FLOOR HALL. "MOUNT PLEASANT"

PALLADIAN WINDOW. SECOND FLOOR HALL.
"MOUNT PLEASANT"

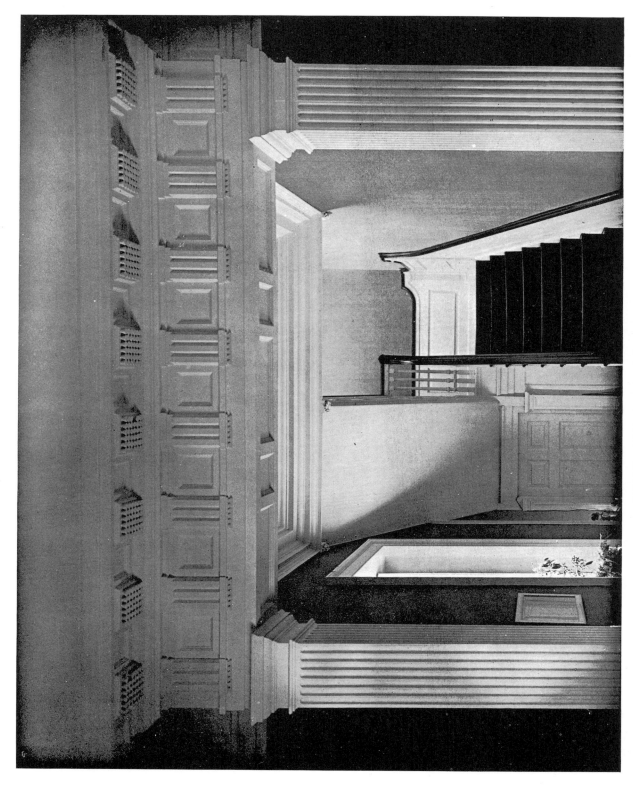

DETAIL. ENTRANCE TO STAIR HALL
"MOUNT PLEASANT"

DETAIL OF DOORWAYS. "MOUNT PLEASANT"

DOORWAY TO EAST BEDROOM
"MOUNT PLEASANT"

EAST BEDROOM. "MOUNT PLEASANT"

NORTH ELEVATION OF PARLOR
"MOUNT PLEASANT"

SOUTH ELEVATION OF PARLOR
"MOUNT PLEASANT"

ENTRANCE HALL TO PARLOR
"MOUNT PLEASANT"

WAINSCOT. PARLOR

"MOUNT PLEASANT"

DETAIL OF FIREPLACE. PARLOR

SECOND FLOOR HALLWAY. LOOKING NORTH. "MOUNT PLEASANT"

DINING ROOM. "MOUNT PLEASANT"

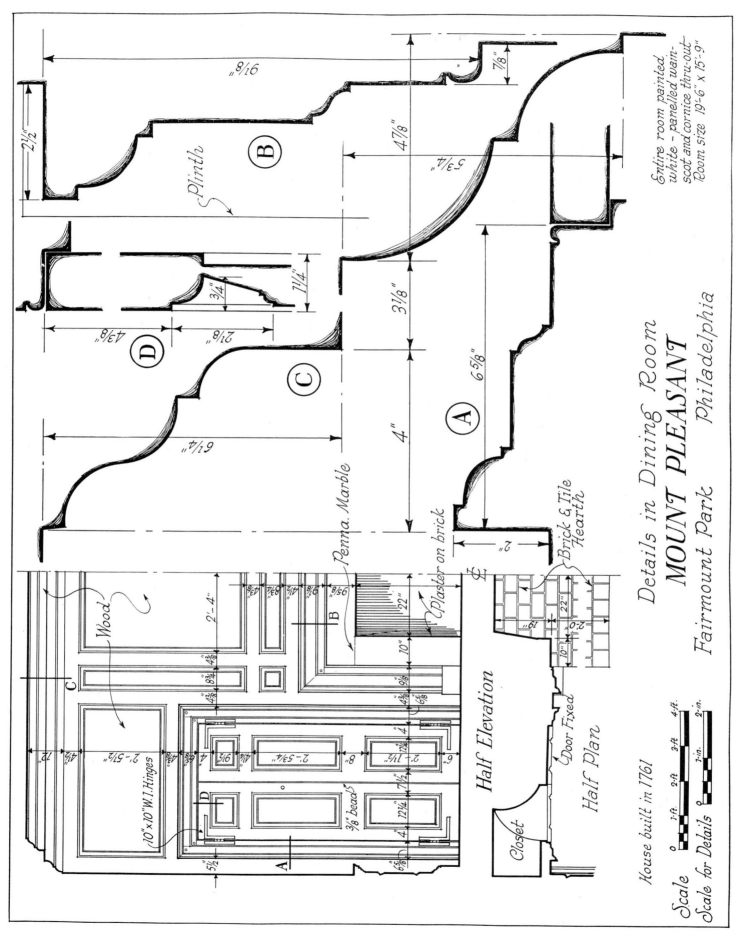

Details in Dining Room
MOUNT PLEASANT
Fairmount Park   Philadelphia

Entire room painted white - panelled wainscot and cornice thru-out
Room size 19'-6" x 15'-9"

House built in 1761

Scale
Scale for Details

LIBRARY. SECOND FLOOR
"MOUNT PLEASANT"

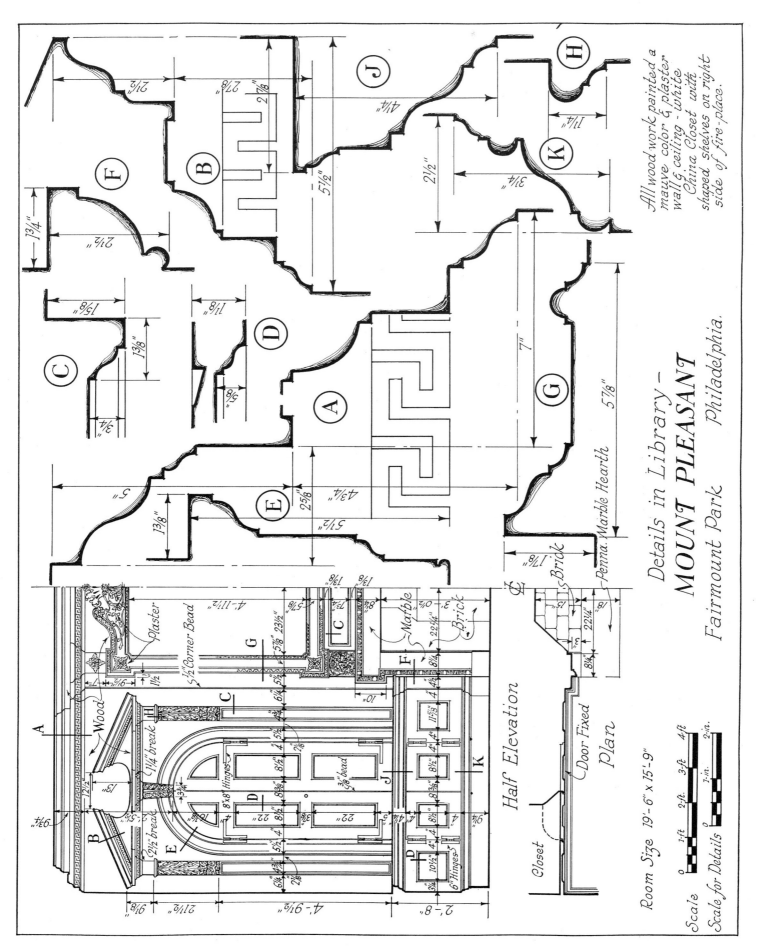

Details in Library –
MOUNT PLEASANT
Fairmount Park   Philadelphia.

All wood work painted a
mauve color & plaster
wall & ceiling - white.
China Closet with
shaped shelves on right
side of fire-place.

Room Size 19'- 6" x 15'-9"

Scale

Scale for Details

Half Elevation

Door Fixed
Plan

Closet

DETAIL OF MANTEL AND CHINA CLOSET. LIBRARY
"MOUNT PLEASANT"

DETAIL LIBRARY. SECOND FLOOR

"MOUNT PLEASANT"

DETAIL OF PALLADIAN WINDOW

"CLIVEDEN" (CHEW HOUSE), GERMANTOWN ROAD

Was built by Benjamin Chew in 1761 as his country seat. The house was occupied by the British in resisting the center of Washington's attack during the Battle of Germantown.

MAIN ENTRANCE "CHEW HOUSE"

ENTRANCE HALL. "CHEW HOUSE"

DOORWAY. ENTRANCE HALL
"CHEW HOUSE"

DETAIL. HEAD OF DOORWAY
"CHEW HOUSE"

DETAIL OF STAIRWAY
"CHEW HOUSE"

STAIR HALL. "CHEW HOUSE"

"THE WOODLANDS" (BLOCKLEY TOWNSHIP), WEST PHILADELPHIA

Was built by William Hamilton, 1770. Like many of the old houses it has two fronts. Extensive gardens surrounded the house. Hamilton introduced the Gingo Tree and the Lombardy Poplar into America.

DETAIL OF WINDOW. "WOODLANDS"

SOUTH ELEVATION. "WOODLANDS"

WEST ELEVATION. "WOODLANDS"

STABLE. "WOODLANDS"

"POWEL HILL," 244 SOUTH THIRD STREET

Was built in 1768 by Chas. Steadman and purchased a year later by Samuel Powel, the last Mayor under the crown and first under the Assembly. The interiors at present repose in the Museums in Philadelphia and New York.

FRONT DOOR "POWEL HOUSE"

Courtesy of Pennsylvania Museum

MUSIC ROOM. "POWEL HOUSE"

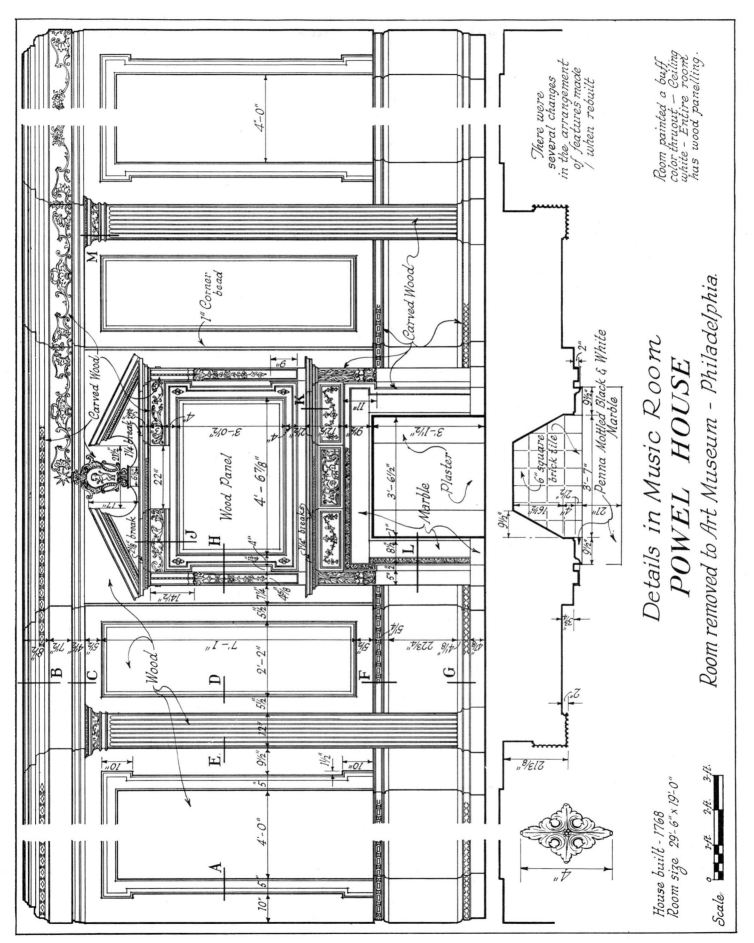

Details in Music Room
POWEL HOUSE
Room removed to Art Museum - Philadelphia.

House built - 1768
Room size 29'-6" x 19'-0"

Scale.

There were several changes in the arrangement of features made when rebuilt

Room painted a buff color thruout - Ceiling white - Entire room has wood panelling.

MANTEL. MUSIC ROOM
"POWEL HOUSE"

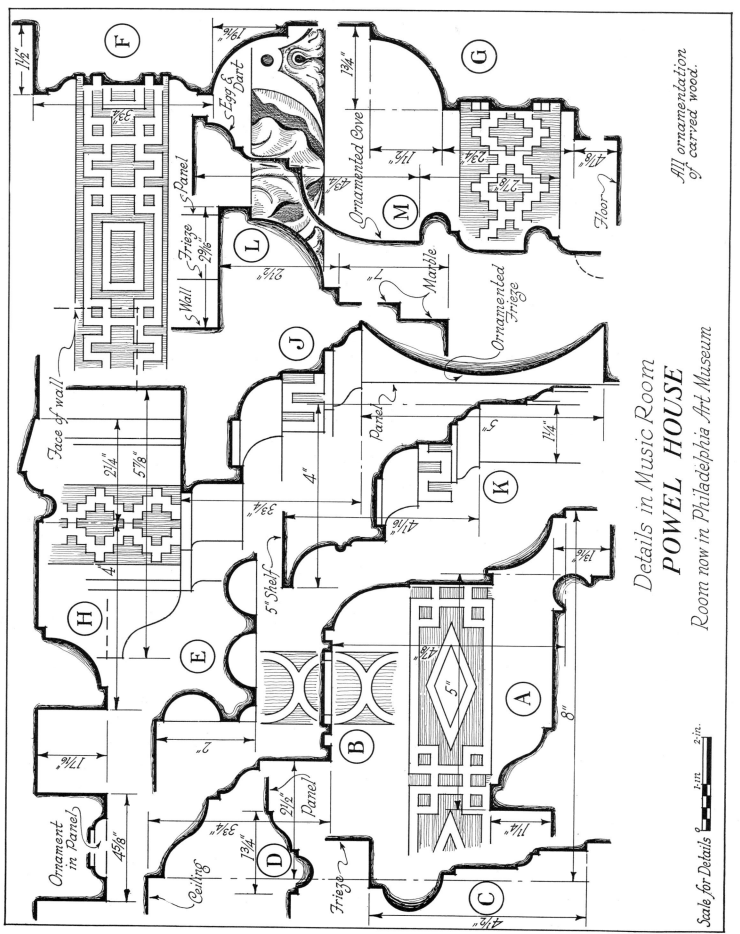

Details in Music Room
POWEL HOUSE
Room now in Philadelphia Art Museum

All ornamentation of carved wood.

Scale for Details

DETAIL OF MANTEL. MUSIC ROOM
"POWEL HOUSE"

DOORWAY IN MUSIC ROOM
"POWEL HOUSE"

PARLOR. SECOND FLOOR
"POWEL HOUSE"

Courtesy Metropolitan Museum of Art, New York City

DETAIL OF MANTEL, MUSIC ROOM (BEFORE REMOVAL)
"POWEL HOUSE"

STAIR LANDING. SECOND FLOOR
"POWEL HOUSE"

STAIRWAY
"POWEL HOUSE"

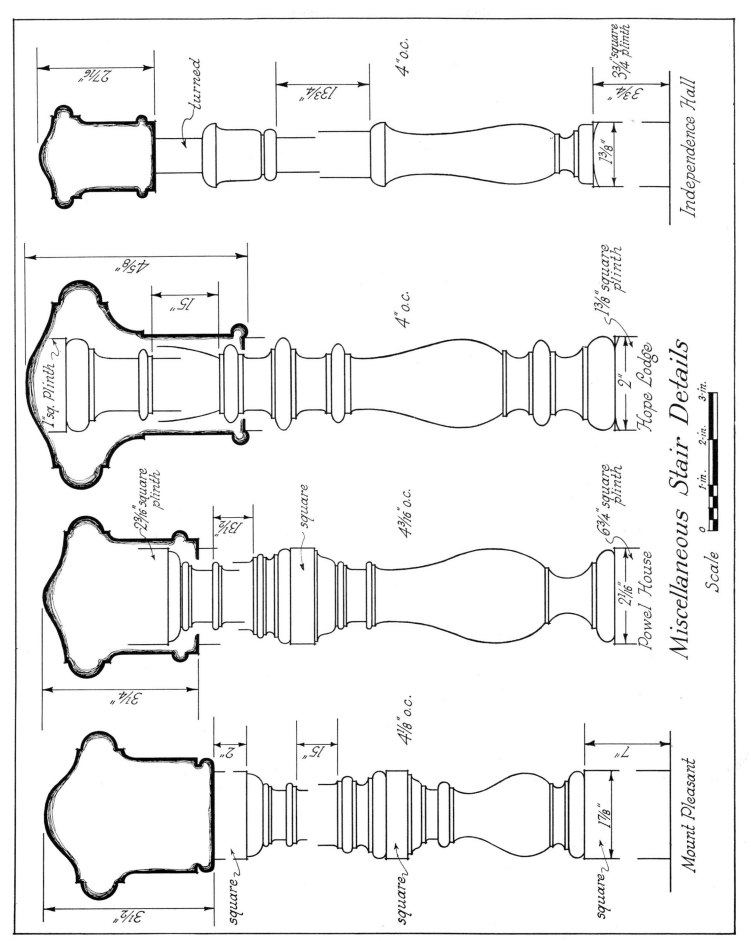

Miscellaneous Stair Details

Scale

Independence Hall

Hope Lodge

Powel House

Mount Pleasant

"WAYNESBOROUGH"

The home of General Anthony Wayne, in the County of Chester, Penna., is situated two miles from Paoli. It is built of brown irregular stone, with a wing at either end. The home was built by Isaac Wayne, 1724.

MAIN DOORWAY. "WAYNE HOUSE"

ENTRANCE HALL. "WAYNE HOUSE"

STAIRWAY. "WAYNE HOUSE"

DRAWING ROOM. "WAYNE HOUSE"

PANELING

HOUSE AT FOURTH AND SPRUCE STREETS, PHILADELPHIA

"BLACKWELL HOUSE," 224 PINE STREET   Detail Door Head
Was built in 1764 by John Stamper, Mayor of Philadelphia in 1759, and purchased by Dr. Blackwell at a later date.

CORNICE DETAILS. "BLACKWELL HOUSE"

"SOLITUDE," (BLOCKLEY TOWNSHIP), FAIRMOUNT PARK

Was built in 1785 by John Penn, a Grandson of the Founder, Wm. Penn. The plaster work is of the finest in the Colonies

ENTRANCE DOOR. "SOLITUDE"

STAIRWAY "SOLITUDE"

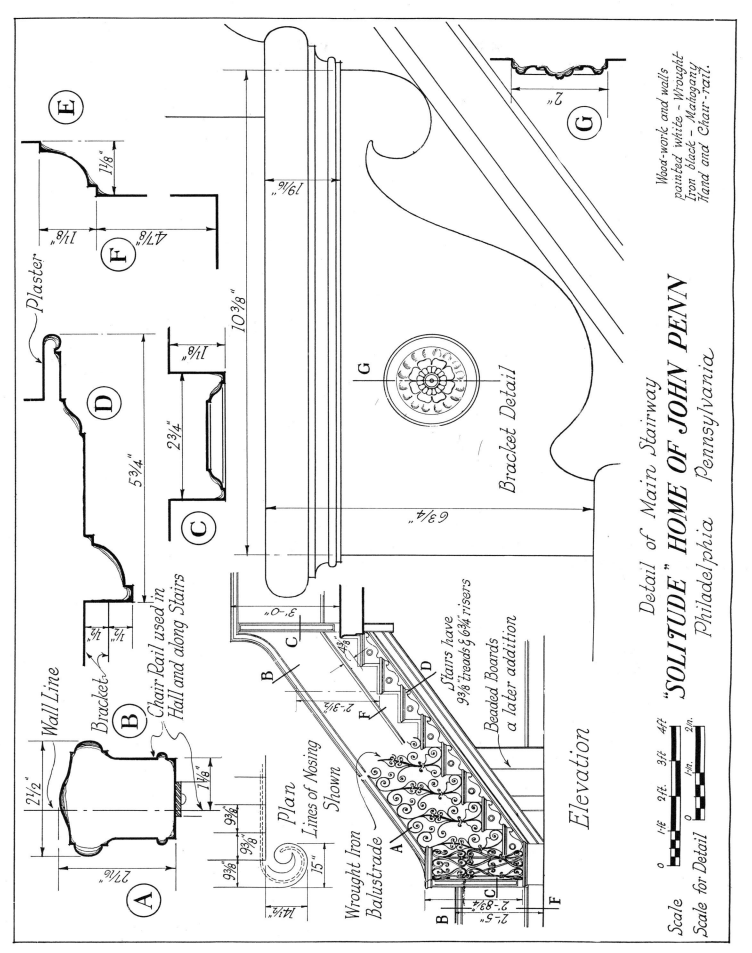

Detail of Main Stairway

"SOLITUDE" HOME OF JOHN PENN

Philadelphia   Pennsylvania

Wood-work and walls painted white – Wrought Iron black – Mahogany Hand and Chair-rail.

Bracket Detail

Elevation

Scale

Scale for Detail

Plan
Lines of Nosing Shown

Wrought Iron Balustrade

Wall Line

Bracket

Chair Rail used in Hall and along Stairs

Plaster

Stairs have 9⅜" treads & 6¾" risers

Beaded Boards a later addition

WINDOW. LIBRARY. SECOND FLOOR

"SOLITUDE"

WINDOW. DRAWING ROOM

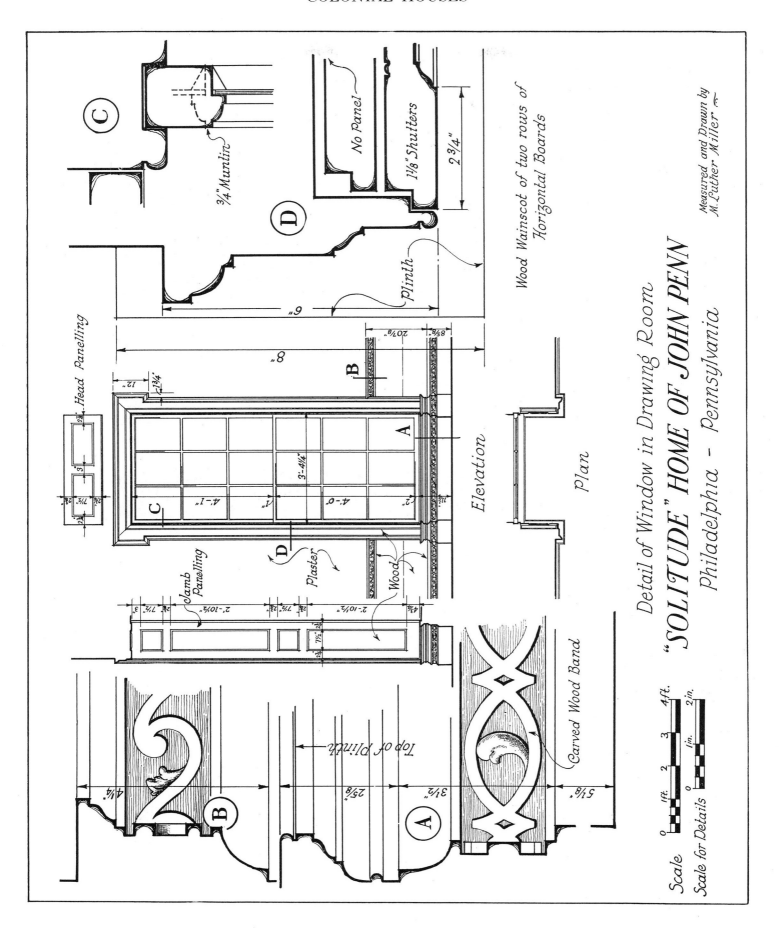

C

D

¾" Muntin

No Panel

1⅛" Shutters

2¾"

Wood Wainscot of two rows of Horizontal Boards

Plinth

6"

Head Panelling

8"

20⅞"

8⅝"

12"

1¾"

2¾"

3"

2½"

B

A

3'-4¼"

4'-1"

1"

4'-0"

1"

2"

1½"

Elevation

C

D

Plaster

Wood

Jamb Panelling

2'-10½"

7½"

3"

7½"

2½"

2½"

4⅜"

Plan

Top of Plinth

Carved Wood Band

B

A

4¼"

2⅝"

3½"

5⅛"

Detail of Window in Drawing Room

"SOLITUDE" HOME OF JOHN PENN

Philadelphia – Pennsylvania

Measured and Drawn by
M. Luther Miller

Scale

Scale for Details

0 1ft. 2 3 4ft.

0 1in. 2in.

DOORWAY. LIBRARY. SECOND FLOOR
"SOLITUDE"

BOOKCASE OVER DOOR. LIBRARY. SECOND FLOOR

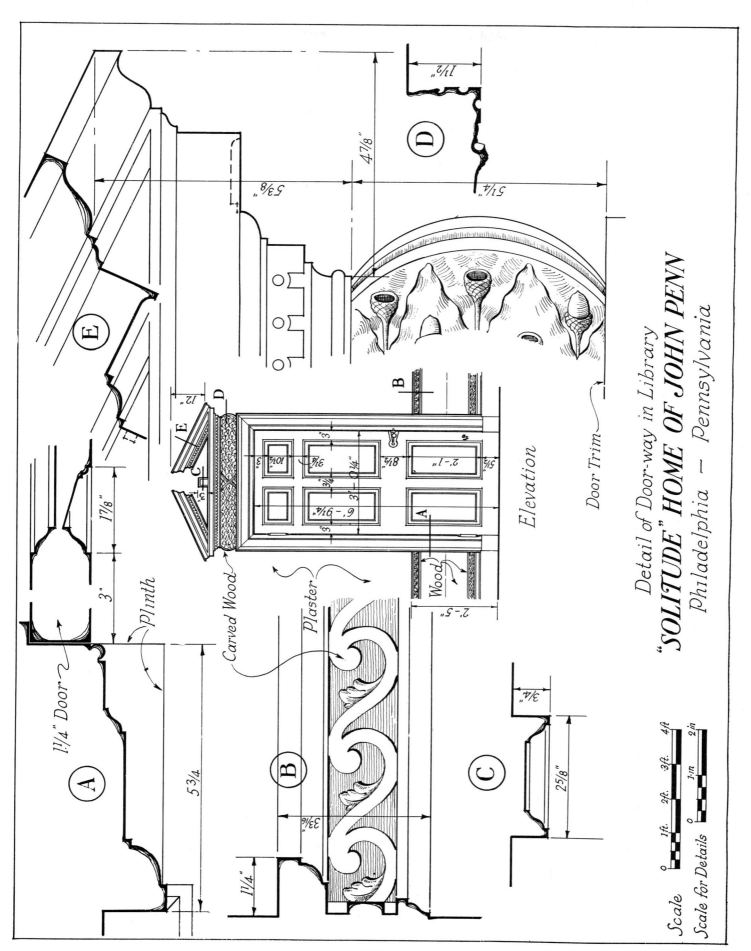

Detail of Door-way in Library
"SOLITUDE" HOME OF JOHN PENN
Philadelphia — Pennsylvania

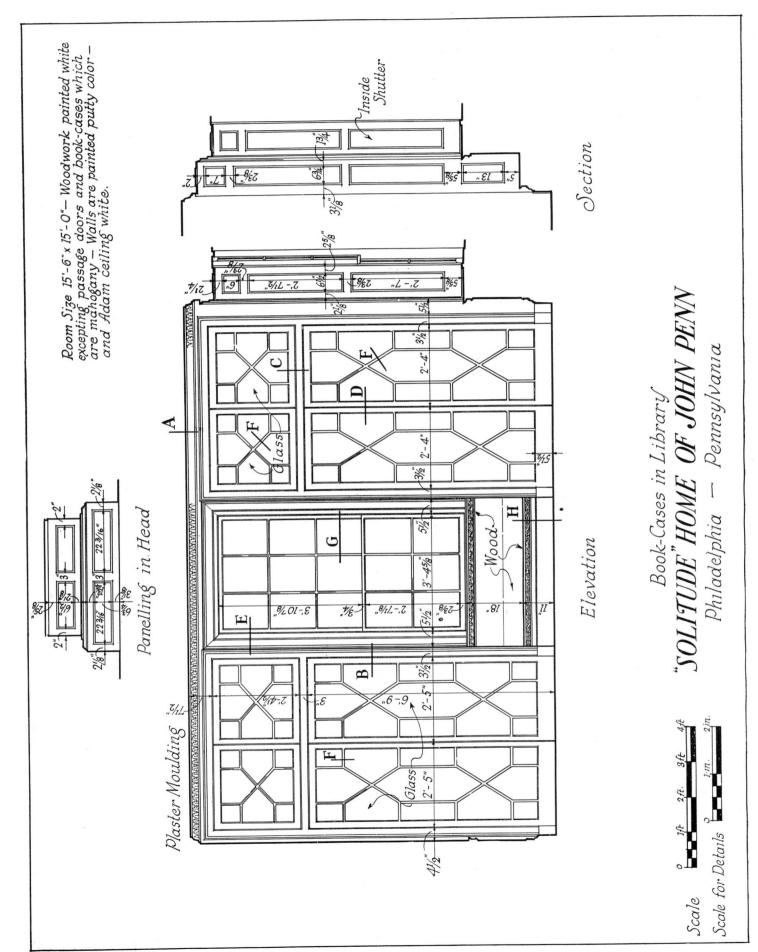

Room Size 15'-6" x 15'-0" — Woodwork painted white excepting passage doors and book-cases which are mahogany — Walls are painted putty color — and Adam ceiling white.

Section

Panelling in Head

Plaster Moulding

Inside Shutter

Book-Cases in Library
"SOLITUDE" HOME OF JOHN PENN
Philadelphia — Pennsylvania

Elevation

Scale

Scale for Details

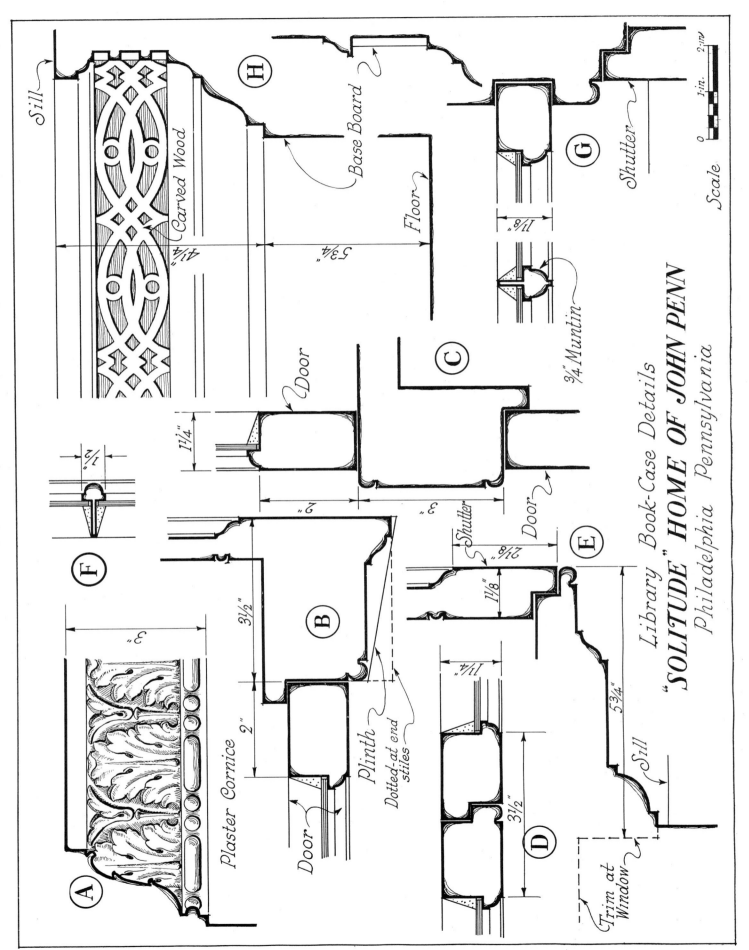

Sill

H

Carved Wood

4¼"

5¾"

Base Board

Floor

G

Shutter

1⅛"

¾" Muntin

Door

1¼"

C

Door

Shutter

2⅛"

1⅛"

Door

E

F

½"

3½"

2"

B

2"

Plaster Cornice

Door

Plinth

Dotted-at end stiles

1¼"

3½"

D

5¾"

Sill

Trim at Window

3"

A

Library Book-Case Details

"SOLITUDE" HOME OF JOHN PENN

Philadelphia Pennsylvania

Scale

0   1-in.   2-in.

PLASTER CEILING. DRAWING ROOM

PLASTER CEILING. LIBRARY. SECOND FLOOR
"SOLITUDE"

PLASTER DETAIL. DRAWING ROOM
"SOLITUDE"

"WICK."   GERMANTOWN, PHILADELPHIA
Built 1692

MAIN ENTRANCE "WICK"

WASHINGTON'S HEADQUARTERS AT VALLEY FORGE

Was built by the Quaker Isaac Potts, Circa 1760; is a two and a half story stone structure. The darkest days of the revolution were spent here by the ragged force of the Continental troops.

DOORWAY. "POTTS HOUSE"

LIVING ROOM "POTTS HOUSE"

DOORWAY. LIVING ROOM. "POTTS HOUSE"

STAIRWAY. "POTTS HOUSE"

DINING ROOM. "POTTS HOUSE"

FRONT BEDROOM. "POTTS HOUSE"

FIREPLACE. CHESTNUT HILL
PHILADELPHIA

THE HERGESHEIMER DOWER HOUSE
Building Started 1713

ENTRANCE DOOR. "DOWER HOUSE"

FIREPLACE. LIVING ROOM
"DOWER HOUSE"

DOOR AND WINDOW DETAIL
"DOWER HOUSE"

LIVING ROOM. "DOWER HOUSE"

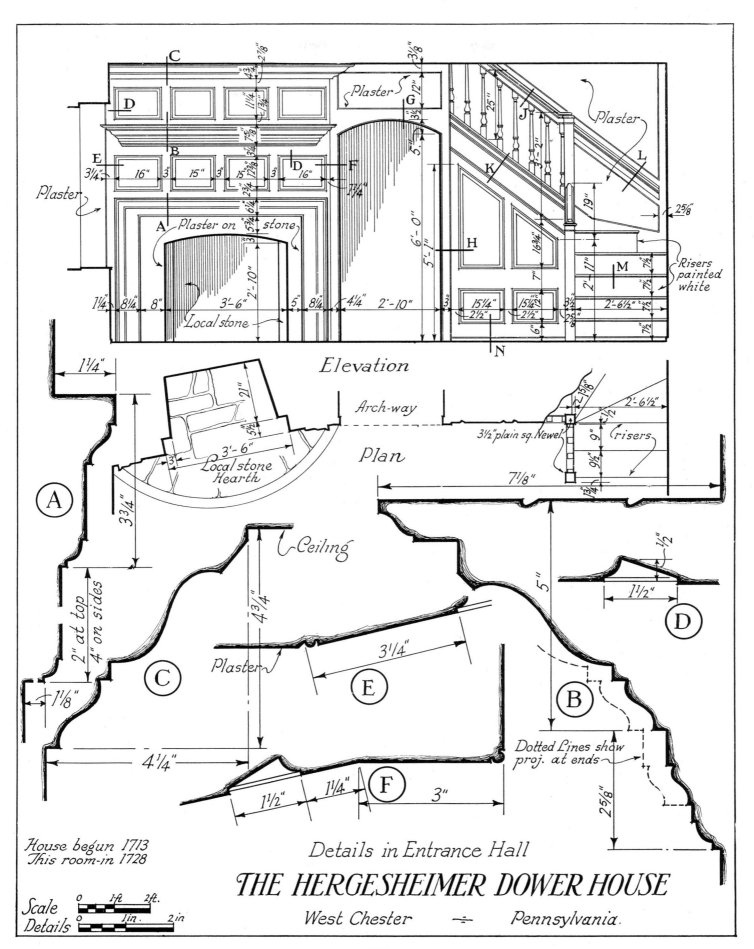

Elevation

Arch-way

Plan

A

C

Ceiling

Plaster

E

F

B

D

Plaster

Plaster on stone

Local stone

Local stone Hearth

3½ plain sq. Newel

risers

Risers painted white

2" at top 4" on sides

Dotted Lines show proj. at ends

House begun 1713
This room-in 1728

Details in Entrance Hall

THE HERGESHEIMER DOWER HOUSE

West Chester — Pennsylvania.

Scale
Details

0   1 ft.   2 ft.

0   1 in.   2 in.

ENTRANCE TO DINING ROOM
"DOWER HOUSE"

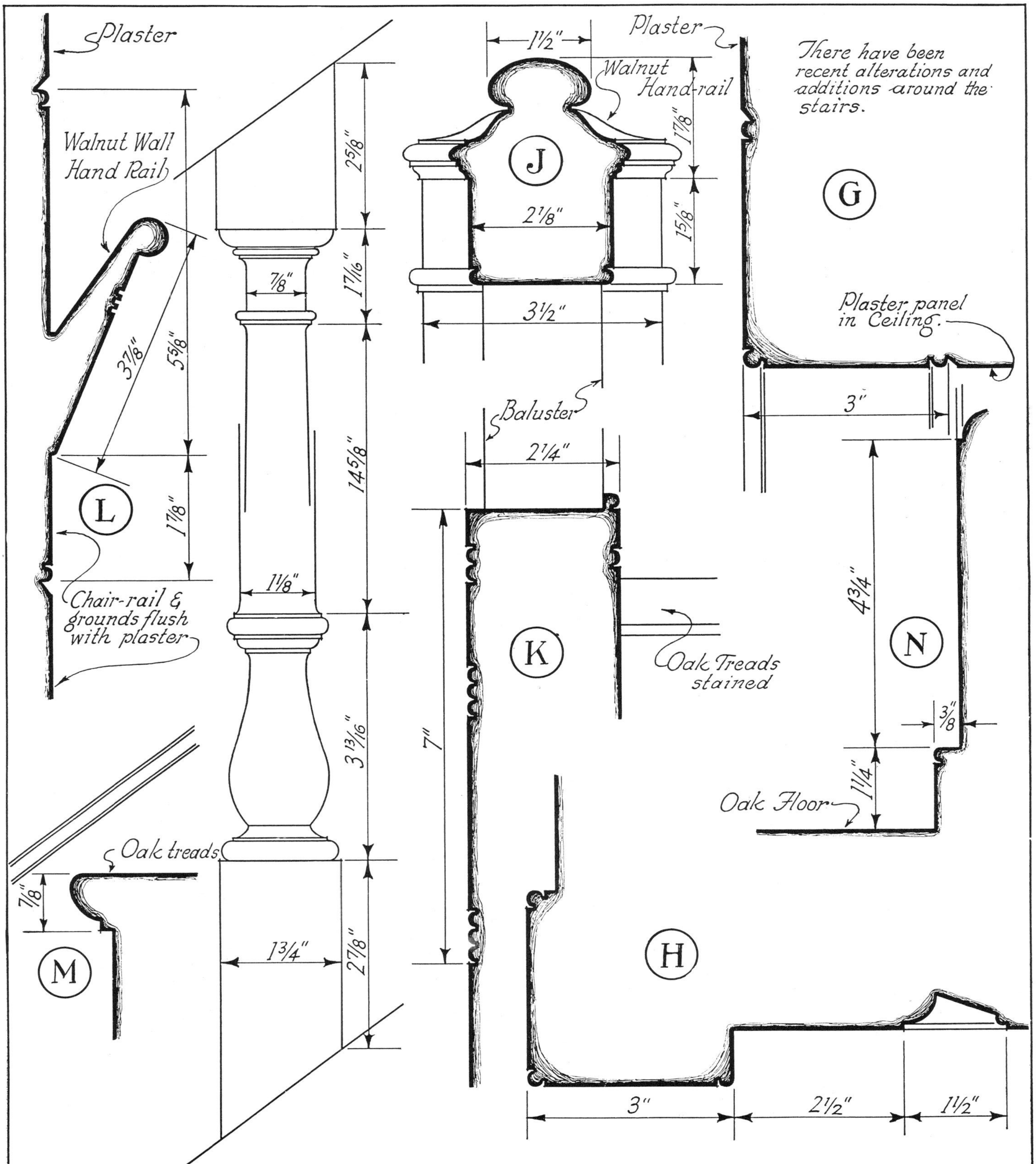
Plaster
Walnut Wall Hand Rail
3⅞"
5⅝"
1⅞"
L
Chair-rail & grounds flush with plaster
2⅝"
7/8"
1 7/16"
14⅝"
1⅛"
3 13/16"
1¾"
2⅞"
Oak treads
7/8"
M
1½"
Walnut Hand-rail
J
2⅛"
1⅞"
1⅝"
3½"
Baluster
2¼"
7"
K
Oak Treads stained
H
3"
2½"
1½"
Plaster
There have been recent alterations and additions around the stairs.
G
Plaster panel in Ceiling.
3"
4¾"
N
3/8
1¼"
Oak Floor

Details in Entrance Hall

THE HERGESHEIMER DOWER HOUSE

West Chester ÷ Pennsylvania.

Scale for Details
0 1-in. 2-in.

Wood-work painted white - Plaster a pale warm grey.

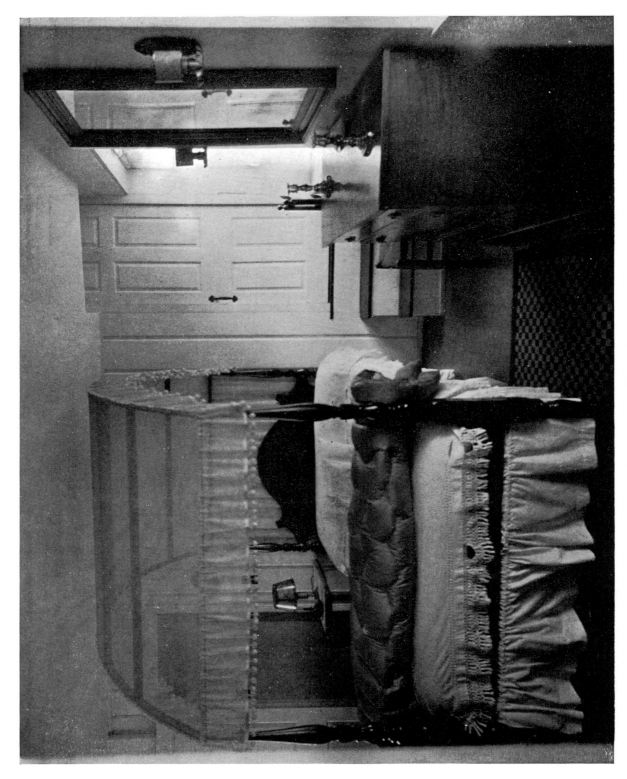

BEDROOM. "DOWER HOUSE"

"STOCKER HOUSE"

404 South Front Street, Philadelphia, was built by John Stocker about 1758.   Mantel detail

MANTEL DETAIL. "STOCKER HOUSE"

MANTEL DETAIL. "STOCKER HOUSE"

MANTEL DETAIL. "STOCKER HOUSE"

MANTEL DETAIL. "STOCKER HOUSE"

MANTEL DETAIL. "STOCKER HOUSE"

"THE CLIFFS"

Situated in Fairmount Park, is a small four room house built by Samuel Rowland Fisher in 1741. The house was occupied at one time by Sarah Boeche, the daughter of Benjamin Franklin.

DETAILS. EAST ENTRANCE DOOR
"THE CLIFFS"

PARLOR. "THE CLIFFS"

DINING ROOM. "THE CLIFFS"

STAIRWAY. "THE CLIFFS"

BEDROOM. SECOND FLOOR
"THE CLIFFS"

BEDROOM. SECOND FLOOR
"THE CLIFFS"

KITCHEN FIREPLACE
"THE CLIFFS"

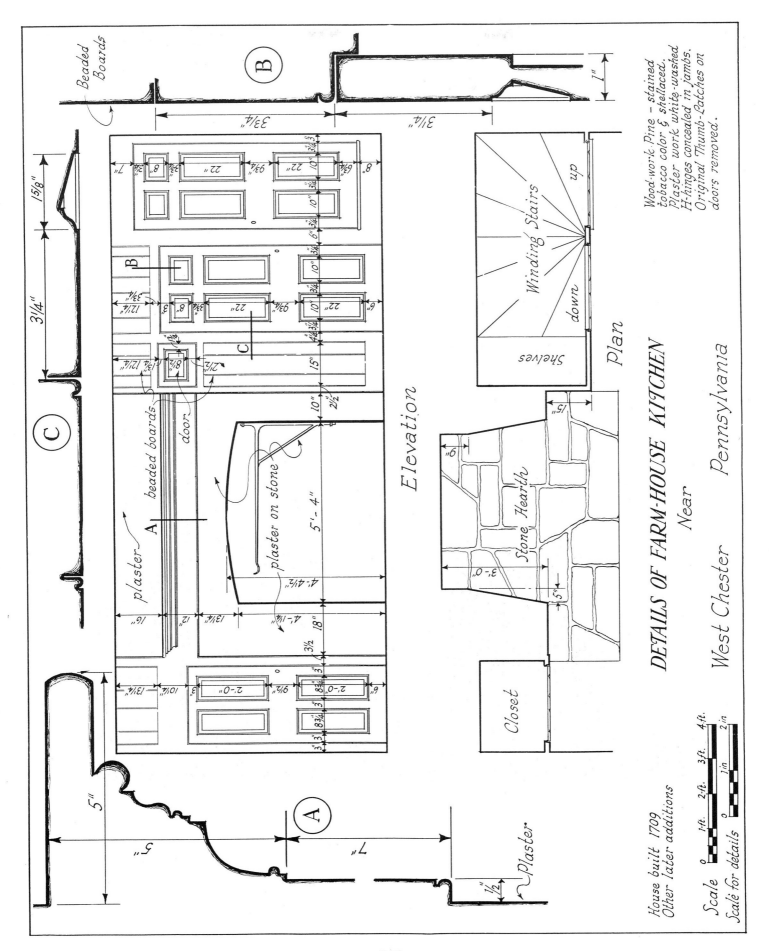

DETAILS OF FARM-HOUSE KITCHEN

Near

West Chester   Pennsylvania

House built 1709
Other later additions

Wood-work Pine - stained
tobacco color & shellaced.
Plaster work white-washed.
H-hinges concealed in jambs.
Original Thumb-Patches on
doors removed.

STAIRWAY TO ATTIC
"THE CLIFFS"

STAIRWAY. "PHILLIPS HOUSE"

STAIRWAY TO CAPTAIN'S WALK
"PHILLIPS HOUSE"

STAIR DETAILS. "PHILLIPS HOUSE"

DETAIL OF STAIR BRACKET
INDEPENDENCE HALL, PHILADELPHIA